17%

D0374805

THE ART OF
ADMINISTRATION

BY

A. LESLIE BANKS, M.A., M.D., F.R.C.P., D.P.H.
BARRISTER-AT-LAW

AND

J. A. HISLOP, M.A., M.D., F.R.C.P. (Edin.)
BARRISTER-AT-LAW

UNIVERSITY TUTORIAL PRESS LTD
9-10 Great Sutton Street, London, E.C.1

Published 1961
Second Edition 1968

SBN: 7231 0452 2

PRINTED IN GREAT BRITAIN BY UNIVERSITY TUTORIAL PRESS LTD, FOXTON
NEAR CAMBRIDGE

PREFACE

THIS book is intended especially for professional men and women coming into contact with the administrative machine for the first time, in the hope that they may thereby be enabled to avoid some of the follies and frustrations so often encountered in this process.

It is based on the joint experience of the authors, who can claim to have served in nearly every type of service described in it, over the past forty years. During that time the pattern of central and local government has undergone many changes. In recent years, for example, there has been a most remarkable development of national services.

The book is concerned essentially with people, and is therefore applicable to all who have to deal responsibly with their fellows. There can be very few indeed who can now claim to have no interest in administration, and all Directors of Education will be well aware of the need for a book of this kind. So, also, will those employed in local and central government service, the administration of hospitals and the social services, voluntary services, nationalised industries, and the public corporations. Even within the universities the burden of administrative work is now heavy.

The authors owe a great deal to the collective wisdom of many colleagues and a list of acknowledgments would be incomplete and invidious. Various sources of reference appear as footnotes to the text, and for those requiring more detailed information a short bibliography will be found at the end of the book.

Thanks are due to the authors and publishers of *Large-Scale Organisation* for permission to reproduce the rules outlined by Sir Geoffrey Heyworth about "The man on the spot".

A. L. B.

Cambridge.   J. A. H.

CONTENTS

CHAPTER I

INTRODUCTION TO
THE ART OF ADMINISTRATION

Those who choose to read the syllabus of a course of training in administration will be struck by the extraordinary degree of subdivision of the subject, amounting almost to fragmentation. Planning, finance, organisation and methods, human relations, and so on, are all separate subjects, or subdivisions of subjects, and one begins to wonder whether there is such a thing as an art of administration.

This doubt is reinforced in the mind of anyone joining a large service for the first time. When he experiences delays and the occasional sense of frustration inevitable with all large administrative machines, his reaction is to find someone on whom to place the blame. To his surprise this is not usually possible, and so he designates some remote or abstract group as "they", and he holds "them" responsible. It is sometimes rather pathetic to find the length to which this process may be carried by otherwise sensible people, for "they" may come to include very large bodies indeed, such as a whole establishment division, the Accountant-General's Department, or even H.M. Treasury. Even more vaguely, the blocks of buildings housing administrative officers may be so designated. Thus, all blame is laid on "Headquarters", or "County Hall", or, classically, "Whitehall".

Equally odd is the way in which a committee of one's fellows, in whose election one has shared, may also become "they", and the Board, the Health Committee, the Finance Committee, and even the staff representatives on a negotiating committee, may be so designated.

There, for many people, the matter rests. They have found a scapegoat and are satisfied. But, if one looks into the matter, the curious fact emerges that "they" are also "us". This hostile and reactionary group, bent on obstructing all our plans, and on refusing our modest demands for money or for essential items of equipment, is apparently made up of quite ordinary people who are neither sadists nor psychopaths. What, then, is the explanation for this curious metamorphosis, whereby these pleasant, easy-going individuals suddenly become rigid bureaucrats when combined together? There are, in fact, two reasons.

1

Firstly, the corporate opinion of a group or committee may commonly be quite unlike that held by the individual members before they sat down together. The extreme example is, of course, where a committee has been called to consider and advise on one matter, and ends up by discussing and making recommendations on something entirely different—a not uncommon experience. It is more usual, however, for the final opinion to represent a compromise of the extreme views. Discussion begins at the opposite poles of the opinions represented and, as the facts become clear, gravitates to the centre. If the chairman and officers of the committee have done their duty, and set the issues and facts clearly before it, the majority of the members, who may never have spoken at all, eventually make up their minds with a remarkable degree of unanimity This careful sifting of the wheat from the chaff is of the essence of the committee system, and the occasional foolishness is merely the exception to the general rule.

The second reason is that "we", rather than "they", are at fault, in that we have failed to keep to the rules, either written or unwritten. In the language of the diplomats, we have failed to observe the protocol. This is very easy to do with the present day spate of regulations, but the professional man is particularly liable to err in this respect. He may be quite unaware that there is any set procedure, but he is more likely to have forgotten it or to regard it as irrelevant. There is also the man who professes a healthy contempt for all rules and regulations, and who regards these as something made by the "clerks" for their own self-glorification.

Some rules can best be honoured in the breach rather than by observance, but, in general, regulations are well-founded. Probably the most common cause of misunderstanding arises over finance. The head of a scientific section or department decides that he must have a new assistant, or a new piece of apparatus, and, naturally, he wants it at once. When asked whether he has made provision for it in his estimates for the coming year, or in the next quinquennium, he indignantly replies that of course he has not for the need has only just arisen. The natural request that he should make a report for the appropriate committee, justifying this new and special expenditure, becomes a source of irritation. If the committee, confronted with half-a-dozen such requests from various sources, decides that they cannot authorise this item, irritation turns to frustration, and to the feeling that the march of science is being deliberately obstructed.

One of the first duties of any newly-appointed head of a scientific or any other division is to find out precisely how the financial machinery works. How much has been allocated and on what basis? Is there any arrangement to meet special contingencies other than petty cash? How are new needs decided and so on?

The Establishment

A word that bewilders the newcomer is the "establishment". To be told that he cannot have extra help because he has his full quota of established staff may mean nothing to him until he learns, slowly and painfully, that the parent organisation can only keep on an even financial keel by deciding in advance how many people it can afford to employ. This it does by a process of allotting a fixed number of workers to each of its various activities. When the number of posts has been agreed upon, and approved, it will then be clear that the total of salaries, and superannuation, and other payments such as family allowances, can be forecast, except for an unforeseen contingency, such as a rise in salaries and wages following some industrial award.

Additions to the permanent staff, even of the most junior of employees, are costly, and, more important, they are an added expense for many years, and possibly for life. For this reason, an attempt suddenly to increase the establishment is treated with reserve, and a "case" must be made out "in writing". Even if there is a strong case (and it is not always so), there may not be enough money to justify all the requests made from various quarters and someone has to do without. This becomes another cause of irritation to the uninitiated.

Temporary staff is usually rather easier to obtain, for there are no permanent commitments in the shape of pension contributions, and the word temporary can come to have quite an elastic meaning, for the person supernumerary to establishment, to quote another difficult phrase, may be carried until a permanent vacancy occurs. What the novice does not always realise, and what, for obvious reasons, the general administrator may not tell him, is that there is often some spare money available because the establishment may not be full. A list of established posts is one thing, but the quota of established people may be rather different, for people die, or resign, or leave to get married, or are transferred temporarily or permanently elsewhere, during the course of the year, leaving a residue of unspent money.

The second duty of the newcomer is, therefore, to find out precisely how many people he has got on his staff, and how many he is entitled to have. When he knows his exact position with regard to finance and staff he is becoming quite knowledgeable, and "they" cease to be so unreal.

The next step is to find out how the general administrative machine works; in other words, "How the wheels go round". If the organisation works in divisions it is necessary to know, broadly, what each division does. If the work is done by committees, then the names and scope of the committees must be determined, and, equally important, how many sub-committees there are, and what they do. Dates of meetings of boards and committees must also be noted. It is useless suddenly to remember some urgent need in the depths of the Long Vacation, or just after the Finance Committee has completed its deliberations for that financial year. Unless these simple precautions are observed the person concerned will earn an unenviable reputation of being either a fool or too sharp. It takes a very clever administrator indeed to break the rules for any length of time, and one should only "play the idiot boy" when it is genuinely necessary to do so.

The next requirement may sound somewhat specious, but it is absolutely essential to know *who* makes the wheels go round. In every kind of organisation, national or local, voluntary or commercial, there is to be found a small handful of people who act as the driving force. This does not mean that they are bundles of energy with sparks coming out of their hair. On the contrary, they are usually quiet and relaxed people, sometimes with a rather weary and disillusioned expression, who apply themselves day in and day out to the supervision of the essential mechanism of the organisation. They need not necessarily be the top people, for the mainspring of a successful office may well be the chief clerk. Similarly, the success of a department may turn, not on the chief on whom the limelight shines, but on the quiet, hard-working deputy whose name is known only to a few.

It is not, therefore, a question of finding out those who matter, with a view to cultivating their good graces, but rather of making sure that one knows the people who do things, for the art of administration is to get things done. The professional man is, by virtue of his training and experience, often ill-fitted to work in administrative harness. The lawyer, accustomed to sifting and weighing evidence and perusing documents, comes nearest to the general administrator, but his training requires him to pay the most meticulous attention to the meaning of words, and to seek for authority in statute and case law, so that he is sometimes regarded as a cold and remote figure who is cautious and conservative in action. He is often more fitted to be the clerk to a local authority, for example, than the aggressive "do it now" administrator of a large industry.

The medical man is probably the least accustomed of all professional people to the administrative reins, for he is concerned with the general personality, the whole physical, mental, and emotional make-up of the human being with whom he is dealing at that moment. He cannot carry over his work until to-morrow, for each problem must be dealt with as it arises, and he has little opportunity to acquire any aptitude for paper work. So accustomed is he to handling sick people, that it comes as something of a shock to him to find that the patient with whom he has been dealing can also be the learned and impartial judge, or the apparently emotionless chairman of a tribunal.

The isolation in which a doctor works, the special nature of his requirements, and the technical language that he uses, all tend to produce a wide gap between medical and lay members of committees, even when these are concerned with medical matters. The layman knows only too well the limitations of his own knowledge, and there is also some truth in the old adage about the devil who "when he was sick a monk would be but when he was well devil a monk was he". Some laymen take an impish delight in scoring off the doctors in administrative matters.

Many people find any form of committee work irksome, partly because they are inexperienced in expressing themselves clearly. The result is that they either sit mute but disapproving, or suddenly burst into such a flurry of indignation that the chairman passes on to the next business as hastily as possible.

Although the medical man has been taken as an example of the difficulties of a professionally trained person in understanding administrative requirements, members of all the professions have somewhat similar experiences. In essence, it amounts to the ability of the technically trained person and the general administrator to develop a common understanding.

It can be said, therefore, that the next administrative requirement to those already noted in this chapter is a common language. The professional expert learns to think in terms of his own particular jargon, whether this be physics, chemistry, or mathematics. The general administrator, for his part, has also his own technical terms, which are second-nature to him but bewildering to others. Fortunately, it is not necessary to try and evolve a new kind of *lingua franca*, for both parties can, if they wish, speak plain English, and technical terms are, or should be, capable of explanation in simple language.

When the expert is asked to make a case in writing for some new need, he should not launch into a highly complex document unless he intends deliberately to befog the issue. A word of warning is necessary here. There is an impression current that one should attempt to overcome any resistance by "blinding with science". This procedure is justified only if the appropriate lay body have exceeded their powers and laid themselves open to attack by venturing opinions on a scientific subject of which they clearly know very little. In these circumstances, the full weight of expert knowledge may be turned loose, provided that it is relevant and accurate. In all other cases plain, simple, forthright statements are best.

There is an art in writing reports and memoranda which is worth the small effort necessary to acquire it. Many men, confronted with a request for information, call immediately for a shorthand writer and begin to dictate. Alternatively, they may seize the microphone of a dictating machine and pour words into it. It used to be said of one eminent man that "he wrote like a dictating machine", and there is no doubt that the man who uses these modern aids can often be recognised by his writings, for they are about one-third longer than they need to be. The purpose of dictation is to get ideas down in a draft, which can then be cut and rearranged in proper order.

Most men find, however, that the best way to write plainly is to marshal their thoughts first in a longhand draft. It may be tedious, and a blank sheet of paper looks ominously like the beginning of an examination, but there is no short cut for the orderly arrangement of past, present, and future. A brief history by way of introduction, a review of the present position, and a reasoned statement of future needs, will leave few loop-holes for criticism, and any rejection of the proposals couched in this manner will call for an equally clear explanation. To leave the matter beyond any doubt it is advisable to summarise the position at the end, and to give a specific statement of what is required. Care should, of course, be taken to ensure that the summary does not meander on until it equals the document in length.

So much for the draft. It must now be sent for typing in draft form, and it is a wise policy not to look at it again that day, but to correct it the next morning. Further drafts may be necessary until the final one expresses clearly and explicitly what is required. As soon as it reaches that stage it should be signed and sent off.

Mention will be made in a later chapter of the need for an efficient office organisation whereby previous correspondence and relevant documents can be found readily, and an orderly routine followed. It is also necessary to emphasise that confidential matters should be so dealt with that they remain confidential. This does not mean only subjects liable to give rise to legal proceedings, but all items of a personal nature. There is nothing more disconcerting or irritating than to find that one's private business is being retailed as general gossip. Everyone is liable at some time or other to find himself involved in distressing, painful, or distasteful circumstances, which often carry a high emotional content. Mental illness, or some peccadillo within the family, may require to be made known to the head of the department or some other senior person. There it should remain, and the organisation should be so designed that information of this kind does not become generally available.

Similarly, correspondence of a personal, private, or confidential nature should be clearly marked as such, both on the letter and the containing envelope, in order that it is not opened by some unauthorised person in the course of the daily routine. It is obviously useless to mark a letter "Confidential" and then to place it in an envelope which is not so marked. Any failure to observe these precautions can give rise to a loss of confidence in the administration, which is very difficult to regain. The administrator who acquires the reputation of being one who cannot be trusted with private information, or who is a gossip, can never hope to be fully informed or fully trusted. A wise old General Inspector of the Local Government Board, when arriving at an institution on which he was to report, would first satisfy himself that all was in order by a meticulous inspection of the books and premises. He would then produce a stubby and unsavoury pipe, light it, and inform the person in charge that "his unofficial ear was now open". Thanks to such "off the record" talks, very few major administrative crises arose in his area.

It follows, from this, that the successful administrator must become a shrewd judge of people. This is largely a matter of experience, but there are certain simple rules which are helpful. It is foolish to expect perfection in anyone, no matter how good he is. Everyone has his Achilles' heel, temporarily or permanently, and there comes a time when personal interests become paramount. For an administrator to give his whole confidence to one person is to invite trouble, for sooner or later illness, a sudden difference of opinion, or some change in personal circumstances, may lead to an estrangement. Many an ideal working partnership has been broken up because, for example, the wives or families have fallen out. No one likes the cold remote guardian of a machine, but the fact remains that the emotions are best left at home, and especially personal likes and dislikes.

Most people work best when their personal interests are at stake, and an enlightened self-interest is often the wisest basis on

which to make a choice. This is particularly important in selecting a man for a special task or in advising anyone on some new
venture. Is it what he wants to do, and, more important, if a
change of environment is indicated, will his wife be contented with
the new surroundings? To post a man to some outlying station
without considering the effects on his domestic life is asking for
disaster, for women are realists, and the vague promise of some
future reward is poor compensation for separation from the pleasant
amenities of life. On the other hand, if it is clearly understood
that the avenue to promotion lies only that way, it is often the wife
who provides the driving force.

There has been much talk, of recent years, about "getting away
from the money incentive", but it is not usually possible to get
very far away from it in the absence of another equally powerful.
Anyone who doubts this should try the simple experiment of finding
out which of two jobs gets finished first, the one which carries a
fee, or the one which does not. In case this sounds unduly cynical,
it should be added that many people are prepared to make reasonable financial sacrifices in order to do interesting work in congenial
surroundings, but it is not every kind of work that comes into this
category, and someone must do the more unpalatable work at some
time or other. It is then that a policy of enlightened self-interest
may prove to be the best for both employer and employee.

From the administrative point of view, people, including members of committees, may be divided broadly into three categories.
There is the group, fortunately the vast majority, who can be relied
upon to agree together in a common-sense manner. Their decisions
may not be entirely in accord with their own personal wishes, but
they are prepared to give and take on details provided that the
broad general principles are safeguarded. There is a much smaller
group of people who can usually be relied upon to take a diametric-
ally opposite view to that of the majority. They are usually strong
individualists with a high degree of intelligence, and their opinions
are well worth having. They are also important, for once in a
while they will insist on the remedying of an injustice, which the
peace-loving majority would allow to pass. Unfortunately, such
people usually like the sound of their own voices, and, as they
become older, the fire within them dies down, and they become
merely nuisances and intolerable bores. Finally, there is the little
group of people whose reactions are quite unpredictable. One day
they will oppose vehemently some course of action, only to agree
equally strongly with something similar at a later date.

It is worth the administrator's while to find out as much as he
can of the background of such people, for they cannot all be written

off as "difficult" or unbalanced. Sometimes the apparently incon
sistent nature springs from a deeply religious sense of conscience,
which makes the person concerned view matters in a light different
from that of his fellows. The position must then be accepted, for
there is no question of arguing with a matter of conscience, and
expediency or compromise cannot be entertained. In other
instances the person concerned takes up his "unpredictable" stance
merely because he is insufficiently informed, and he is then
amenable to preliminary "sounding" and discussion. A few do
it to attract attention, or as part of a set policy of self-advancement.

The embryo administrator would do well to remember that he
must take all these people as he finds them. He cannot alter
human nature, and he must learn to work harmoniously with all
types of persons if he is to succeed in getting things done. This
implies that the person he must know best of all is himself. The
sudden flurries of anger or despair, the desire to "have it out" or
to ride rough-shod, are the experiences of everyone, but they are
best transferred into the refrigerator at the back of one's mind for
twenty-four hours. If at the end of that time it is still apparent
that strong action is required it can be taken, but never on the spur
of the moment.

On the other hand, the administrator who neglects to act
promptly, through indecision or fear of the consequences, when
he knows what he should do, is failing in his duty. This may
sound like a counsel of perfection, as indeed it is, but the whole
purpose of having administrators is to get things done, and they
are in a much more favoured position in this respect than their
professional colleagues, for they can take time to seek the best
advice before they act. The surgeon cannot stop in the middle
of an operation, or the barrister while in court, to reconsider the
problem, whereas the administrator can consult various authorities. Once the course of action is clear, however, he must be prepared to act firmly and definitely. In order to be able to do so
he must have sufficient time to "think the matter out", and that
is where many administrators fail. Their time is so taken up with
details that the unusual problem becomes unwelcome. Anyone can
go through the motions of administration, the routine letters, the
stock answer on the telephone, the promise to "look into" the
matter, but it is the hallmark of the master-craftsman that he can
delegate these to others, and take the major problems to himself.

So far, the requirements for skill in administration have been
listed as an accurate knowledge of facts, and a skilled assessment of people, including oneself. There is one other requirement
—a steadfast belief in the value and importance of the work to be

done. Mastery of the techniques is not enough, and many people will be familiar with the skilled administrator who is merely going through the motions, such as the elderly man trained in a different service who is transferred to some undertaking in which he is not particularly interested. The wheels revolve smoothly, but the spirit, or fire, is lacking. Unless there is a firm and constant belief in the value and importance of the work to be done, administration can become dull, mechanical, and uninspired.

What is it that makes for success in the gentle art of administration? It is certainly not merely the observance of rules, nor the exercise of authority, for in that event the ideal pattern of administration would be that of a well-run gaol. Nor is it at the other extreme outlined in Pope's couplet: —

"For forms of government let fools contest,
Whate'er is best administered is best."

Some of the essential requirements have already been noted. All concerned, administrators and administrees, so to speak, must believe that the thing to be administered is worth the effort involved. Similarly, those who administer any service must have the confidence of the people who work in it, and the basis of this mutual trust is a common understanding.

Both sides have a duty to forestall misunderstandings, and to seek explanations directly they arise. In order to be able to do this they must speak a common language. The danger lies in faulty reasoning because of insufficient knowledge. The administrator may assume, for example, that the specialist has said all there is to say, whereas, in fact, there may be considerable gaps in the available knowledge about that particular matter. The layman finds it hard to believe that in professional practice there can be no such word as "never" (or hardly ever, as the captain of "H.M.S Pinafore" would say). The professional experts, on the other hand, may fail to realise how tightly the general administrator's hands are tied financially, with all that follows from this in the way of limitation of equipment and staff.

If the people in it disapprove of the administration of a service, the remedy does not lie in sullen silence and obstruction, or in impassioned letters to the press. It becomes necessary to see that things are put right, and the people to do this are those most closely concerned. If matters are allowed to drift until some independent outside body is called in, the cure may prove to be very drastic indeed. It would be much better for everyone to acquire some knowledge of the principles of administration. If they do not choose to do this but to "leave all that to the clerks", they will get the kind of service they deserve.

They will qualify, also, for a paraphrase of W. S. Gilbert's gibe : —

> "Administration we bar,
> It is not our bent,
> On the whole we are
> Not intelligent."

CHAPTER II

THE SELECTION AND CONTROL OF STAFF

Much has been written about the selection of staff, and attempts have been made, from time to time, to devise scientific methods whereby the element of chance may be minimised. Some of these methods depend on a kind of "points" system, whereby certain standards of education, reliability, integrity, and similar factors, can be assessed.

A great deal depends, of course, on the type of work concerned. For routine duties which do not involve much responsibility it is possible to lay down certain standards, but for more responsible work the question of personality arises, and this becomes increasingly important with the more senior posts.

There are certain basic requirements in making a selection for any type of work. Physical fitness for the work to be performed is, for example, of great importance. Some duties can be performed by severely handicapped persons, such as the blind, the deaf, or the crippled, but even here care must be exercised. Epilepsy, formerly regarded with horror by employers, is now known to be controllable by medical care, and epileptics can be safely employed in a great variety of undertakings, but common sense would dictate that they should not engage on work requiring them to climb ladders, or to tend moving machinery, or to drive certain types of vehicles unless certified as medically fit to do so.

Medical Examination

A medical examination before permanent employment is usually insisted upon by all large undertakings. It serves a double purpose, for it ensures that the applicant is physically fit, so far as can be ascertained, for the proposed work, and it also acts as a safeguard for the health of the other workers by ensuring that there is no question of some transmissable disease, such as pulmonary tuberculosis, being present. Some employers require an X-ray examination of the chest as a further safeguard in this respect.

When requesting a medical report on any person it is necessary to specify the precise nature of the work likely to be involved, so that the doctors may know to what points they should pay particular attention. This is essential where heavy manual work is involved, but it is also important in certain occupations, such as driving public service vehicles, where mental stability is of major importance.

It is not enough for the layman merely to enquire "Have you had any serious illness?" and be satisfied with a shake of the head, for there are different kinds of serious illnesses. Some are of short duration and leave no ill-effects, while others are of long-standing with a tendency to recur. The final decision must rest with a medical man, but it is a safe generalisation to say that any history of an illness lasting for three months or longer should be investigated further.

A doctor can forecast, with a high degree of accuracy, the physical fitness of any given person for employment. He can also, if asked, make a reasonably accurate assessment of the mental and emotional stability of the person before him, but he cannot be expected to furnish a detailed psychological report unless he has special training or experience. There is, in any event, no general touchstone, for psychological enquiries must be related to the work in question. The requirements for an entrant to the higher Civil Service, for example, would be very different from those of a pilot who is to fly jet aircraft.

An advantage of medical examination on entry which is not always appreciated is that it acts as a valuable check in the event of subsequent illness, and especially if a claim for compensation arises. Concealment of a previous disability is not unknown, and a statement that a disease has been contracted in the course of employment might be difficult to controvert in the absence of a medical examination on entry.

Equally important is the standard of education reached by the candidate. At first sight it would appear a simple matter to say "we will take only university graduates" or "a minimum of three 'A' levels in . . .", but, in the first place, the work may not require, or it may not satisfy, people of this standard, and, in the second place, they may not be suitable for the work although they possess the necessary paper qualifications. A university degree, or a diploma, or a certificate, may mean merely that the candidate has, at some given time, satisfied the examiners of his ability to answer certain questions. He may at the moment of the examination have reached a standard far above his normal capacity. On the other hand, he may have failed miserably to do justice to his natural abilities. In any event, it is necessary to consider academical attainments in relation to the work involved.

The old system of personal selection by the head of the department concerned, followed by a period of "in-service" training or "learning by doing", is rapidly being superseded by selection boards and committees which are, in turn, governed largely by the special or technical qualifications required for the work under consideration.

Thus, in various aspects of social work, the general worker formerly recruited on personal aptitude is now being replaced by those who have undergone some special course of training, and who possess certificates or diplomas to this effect.

Testimonials and References

There will always remain, however, the third element in selection, namely, personal and social suitability for employment, and the ability to fit in with the rest of the team. This requirement can be assessed only by previous enquiry supplemented by personal interview. Previous enquiry is usually made in the form of testimonials and references.

Testimonials are written with the knowledge that the candidate will see them, and are therefore of less value than references. Nevertheless, much can be learned from them if examined intelligently. It is advisable to study them in the light of the previous experience of the candidate, and those which are out-of-date, or which do not cover recent employment, should be regarded with some measure of reserve. Similarly, those which are couched in formal or general terms, or are merely lukewarm, should be examined with care. On the other hand, a testimonial written especially for the post in question by a competent person, and recommending the candidate unreservedly for employment, can usually be taken at its face value.

Many employers now prefer to ask a candidate to submit the names of referees to whom application may be made. An essential requirement, often neglected, is for the applicant to ask the proposed referee if his name may be given in this way. There are several reasons why the referee may not wish his name to go forward. He may not have a very high opinion of the individual concerned and may be forced to say so, in which case it would be much better not to give his name. He may know that the work proposed is not suitable for the candidate and advise him accordingly. More difficult is the position where several people propose to nominate the same referee. This happens not uncommonly in local government work, and it would be generally agreed that it is the duty of the referee to speak as fairly of each candidate as he humanly can. It would be wrong of such a man to refuse a request merely because someone else had asked first, because he would thereby be prejudging the issue, but the fact remains that several favourable references from the same employer for one post may weaken the claims of all. If consulted by the applicant in advance, a referee may reasonably intimate that he has already been asked by someone else, without divulging names.

Once a referee has promised to act he must speak fairly, honestly, and fully. It is a good plan to begin by saying how long one has known the candidate, and in what capacity, before proceeding to analyse his professional skill and ability and personal character. The reference should end, if possible, with a clear and unambiguous recommendation, with or without reservations, for the post under consideration. Members of selection committees are only human, and they tend to seize on some disparaging comment. If there is any doubt as to the meaning of the reference the writer should be asked to clarify it.

The candidate may be interviewed either before or after taking up references, according to the responsibility involved in the work. For the routine grades of worker, interview may precede the taking up of references, but for executive and administrative posts it is desirable to make full enquiry beforehand, so that the selecting body may have all relevant information before it.

There is an art in submitting applications. Anyone who has had experience in wading through large numbers of these will recognise at once the feeling of relief with which a certain type of application is greeted, as compared with the distaste for the jumbled mass of verbiage in others, in which every relevant fact has to be sought for separately. If there is no form of application, the candidate should begin by saying who he is, where he lives, how old he is, and whether he is married or single. Where appropriate the number of children should be stated. Next should follow, in chronological order, but with the minimum of words, the *curriculum vitae*, so that the selectors may see at a glance the previous history, school, university, military service, previous and present employment, and so on. The application may conclude with a brief statement of why the candidate wants to do the work in question, and drawing attention to any special qualifications and experience which he thinks may render him particularly suited for it. There is no objection to beginning the chronological table with the present employment and working backwards, if this seems to put the candidate's experience in a better light. The thing to avoid, at all costs, is launching into a detailed description of the importance of the job for which application is being made, and a platitudinous commentary on one's own peculiar aptitude for it. The selectors know precisely what the job is worth, and also the type of person they are looking for, and they do not need to be told.

Interviews

If there are many applications for a post it is customary to make a short list of those deemed suitable for interview, and an element of unfairness may enter here quite unwittingly. If there is a time-limit for entry it should be observed, and late-comers considered only if there are special circumstances. There is a certain type of applicant who really only wants a day's excursion and his travelling expenses, and another who may apply merely in the hope of forcing the hand of his present employers to improve his position. If all applications are arranged and examined carefully in alphabetical order no harm can be done to anyone, whereas haphazard selection, or "dipping", may result in the practised writer catching the eye to the detriment of the genuine candidate.

Members of selection committees are sometimes asked to make a short list "in order of merit". This is not a very desirable procedure, for it may prejudice in advance of interview the chances of the man who is unskilled in making out his application. It is preferable to arrange a short list in alphabetical order. The interview can also be taken in this order without arousing a sense of unfairness among the candidates, for those whose names begin with X, Y, and Z are accustomed to waiting, and they have the consolation, for what it is worth, of knowing that the impression made by A, B, or C may have faded by the time their turn comes.

The purpose of interview is, or should be, to select the most suitable candidate for a particular post, and it requires the consideration of many other matters than mere academic ability. The candidate with high academic distinction may prove to be temperamentally unfitted for this work, whereas the person with apparently inferior attainments, on paper, may reveal qualities of courage, independence, and initiative which are precisely those which may be required. It is important, therefore, that the interview should be so conducted as to elicit information of this kind.

As always, much depends on the chairman if the interview is conducted by a committee. It is his responsibility to see that adequate time is allowed for each candidate, and that the latter is put at his ease. Each member of the committee should be given the opportunity to put questions, and the candidate should be given the opportunity to speak in answer to the final question, "Have you anything you would like to ask us?". It is desirable, at an interview, to enquire into any gaps in the written application, such as periods of time which are unexplained or an illness of uncertain nature or duration, but, in general, each interview for a given appointment should follow similar lines so that candidates (who almost invariably compare notes afterwards) may not get the impression that they have been unfairly treated. Candidates, for their part, should avoid certain pitfalls, such as an air of over-confidence, or talking too much. Many a man has "talked himself out of a job", and committees tend to distrust an excess of self-assurance.

Although the formalities of written application, the taking up of references, personal interviews, and a medical examination are the common pattern of selection, this procedure must vary with the nature and importance of the post concerned. The highest administrative and judicial posts, requiring exceptional experience and personal qualities, are commonly filled by invitation, for the field of selection is small, the individuals well known, and any form of competitive application would be invidious. Senior officials in local government and similar services are recruited by open advertisement, and with the most meticulous care to ensure that there can be no suggestion of graft or nepotism. It is the custom to declare explicitly that canvassing will disqualify. For example, Standing Orders may say that "Canvassing of members of the Board or any Committee of the Board for any appointment under the Board shall disqualify the candidate for such appointment". Similarly, candidates are expected to disclose whether they are related to any member of the committee or to the holder of any senior office. "A candidate who purposely and deliberately conceals such information shall be disqualified for such appointment and, if appointed, shall be liable to dismissal without notice." Any member of the employing body or senior officer must also disclose such relationship with the candidate, and the comments made elsewhere in this book on the "interest" of members apply here equally as in the case of contracts.

In the appointment of minor executive, clerical, and manual staff, it is common practice to leave the selection to one individual, usually the head of the department or section concerned, provided that he is able to satisfy the employing body that the person selected has the required qualities, educational level, and medical fitness for employment. Even here, however, the principles outlined above hold good. The appointment must not only be fair and just; it must also be clearly seen to be so.

A rather heavy responsibility rests on the individual responsible for selections of this kind, for it is in repetitive employment that the trouble-maker has most opportunity. At this level, personal interest in the work, and incentives to plod on day after day, may be relatively few, and personal likes and dislikes assume an importance out of all proportion to their true value. It is in applications for this class of employment, also, that the flotsam and jetsam of life may be found, and a ready tongue and a gentlemanly bearing may mask the psychopathic personality or the embittered failure. Hence the need for the most careful enquiry into antecedents. It is necessary to look especially at testimonials which are too glowing, for there may be an urgent desire on the part of the donor to "speed the parting pest".

Anyone who has been much concerned with the selection of staff will recognise and sympathise with an instinctive feeling of warmth towards a particular candidate, and the conviction that he is the "right" person. Often it turns out to be so, but it is as well to be on guard against an emotional selection, unless approved by others also, and unless there is a good solid foundation of ability in the candidate to support it.

Where the rules permit of it, employment for a trial period has many advantages, particularly where a certain degree of technical skill is required, as promise and performance do not always match. The typist claiming to be capable of a certain speed and accuracy can be tested forthwith, but this is not the case with many other classes of employees whose aptitude can only be assessed over a period of months.

There is always much talk of selecting "the job for the man" and not the man for the job, but relatively little attention is paid to selection for a given set of working conditions. Thus, a woman may fit well into a masculine society, but it is only exceptionally that a man can adapt himself to work entirely in a feminine one. Generally, it is wiser, given two candidates of equal ability, to choose a man to work with men and a woman to work with women. With the increasing numbers of older people in employment, it is desirable to pay some regard also to the age structure when making a selection. Where the rest of the staff are mainly young the effects of introducing an older person, except in a supervisory capacity, require careful thought. This is particularly the case with women, for the interest of young and old are entirely different, and they tend to irritate each other, whereas young men seem to respect the experience of older men, and work reasonably well with them.

This question of relating selection to working conditions applies to the control of staff. If working conditions are good, and the work interesting and varied, the main pre-occupation of the administration should be to select suitable people and then leave them alone. Women, again, are capable of long spells of routine repetitive work without boredom and maintain a high standard of accuracy, provided that their surroundings and their companions are pleasant, whereas men engaged on similar work would tend to become irritable and inattentive. It is not always realised that many people do not want personal responsibility, but prefer to be able to escape to their homes and hobbies at a set time each day. This is true of many women, not because they are incapable of the additional effort, but because it does not appeal to them.

With a carefully selected and contented staff the question of control, in the sense of regimentation, should not arise, but there are certain pitfalls that the administrator must be careful to avoid. One of the most important of these is any semblance of partiality or favouritism. Everyone with experience of working in a service will remember the "blue-eyed boy" who can do no wrong, or, even worse, the type of chief who has a succession of "blue-eyed boys". It is an unhealthy situation in many ways, for it commonly implies that the administrator, or head of the department or section, has either lost confidence in some members of his staff or in himself. The arrival of a young, keen, and ambitious newcomer provides the opportunity to use him as a personal assistant to search out information, check references, and prepare drafts on which the great man can base his own reports. From this innocent beginning it is only a short step to that of personal confidant, and from there to general informant on staff and office matters.

One of the disadvantages of increasing administrative responsibility is that of loneliness. Indeed, there is some resemblance between the successful administrator and the mountaineer. Both must, of necessity, be good climbers, and the higher they go the fewer in number become their companions, until they reach the cold and solitary summit. This sense of isolation is particularly evident where the administrative head has been brought in from outside and is thus a stranger to the staff, who may, not unnaturally, be resentful of this new obstacle to their own promotion. Such a man may turn the more readily to the new arrival for assistance, with the chain of events described above. The results can be most unfortunate for all concerned. The staff become suspicious and watchful, and the cleft between them and the head widens. The newcomer finds himself fawned upon or insulted, depending on the temperament of the individuals with whom he deals, and a whole chain of tortuosities and obliquities, and of little petty politics, may develop. All this may sound somewhat far-fetched, but it can happen, and when it does the working efficiency of the unit may suffer severely. It is not very long, in such circumstances, before someone finds an opportunity to inform the chairman or other members of the governing body that all is not well and, as the saying goes, "mud sticks", and memories are long, particularly in large services.

Almost as serious as this error of commission is that of omission, by which is meant the deliberate by-passing of a responsible official. It may be, for example, that the second in command or chief clerk is not up to his work, or is old and hidebound, or that a personal antipathy develops between chief and deputy. This situation is particularly likely to arise with the introduction of a new administrative head. The natural tendency is to short-circuit and avoid as much as possible any contact with the resistant and difficult one. This policy is short-sighted, because it does not take into account the effect on the staff as a whole, many of whom may have a deep sense of loyalty to the man they know, and a feeling of sympathy for his being passed over for promotion. It is also bad because it wastes the experience and working capacity of the individual concerned. There are occasions, of course, when the situation may be quite impossible, and drastic action is required in the form of retirement, transfer elsewhere, or even down-grading, but these courses are not lightly to be undertaken, and the situation must manifestly be seen by all concerned to be irremediable before they can be followed.

Except in the case of personal antipathy, or of unfitness for the work, it is usually possible to arrive at a solution to the problem by means of trial and error. Where there are personal antagonisms it is the duty of the administrative head to consider, quite dispassionately, his responsibilities as a whole. If he can, without loss of dignity, make the first move towards improved relations he should do so, and unless the person he is dealing with is psychologically abnormal, he should, with patience, be successful. The thing to avoid, at all costs, is the state of affairs where chief and deputy communicate with each other only in writing. The position of the rest of the staff then becomes quite intolerable, for they never know to whom to turn for advice. For people in responsible administrative positions to adopt habitually this method of communicating with each other is an indication of lack of confidence, to say the least.

Possibly the greatest failing in an administrative head is the inability to make and enforce a decision, particularly if it is likely to be unpalatable. Differences of opinion arise among the most intelligent of staffs, frequently over quite trivial matters. Often the wisest course is to turn a blind eye and leave them to adjust themselves, but once in a while the matter requires to be settled authoritatively, and that is what the chief is there to do. The old legal maxim, *audi alteram partem*, applies. Both sides must be heard, either separately or together, and, after due thought, a firm decision must be given and adhered to. Any semblance of weakness or wavering can have a most disturbing effect on the confidence and peace of mind of the staff, who are left with a feeling of insecurity.

Failure to delegate responsibility can also have serious effects on morale, even in a small office. There is a certain type of man who has hitherto been successful only because he has attended to every detail personally. His reputation for industry and reliability has become high, and he finds himself selected to administer a staff. His natural tendency is to want to retain everything in his own hands, to see every incoming letter and to see and sign every outgoing one, to peruse and amend all drafts, and to have every administrative problem, however trivial, referred to him. The effect on his subordinates is usually most unfortunate, for they become merely passive. In the course of time the ambitious ones go elsewhere, and he is left with those who tolerate or prefer routine work without responsibility.

Such a man can build up a mountain of paper work, which eventually collapses and suffocates him. It is well known, for example, that letters breed letters, and it is possible so to increase one's correspondence that it becomes the major pre-occupation of the day. Furthermore, the man who cannot delegate must proceed by way of written requests within his office for facts, figures, statements, and the like until he becomes so busy that he can never leave his desk. It is obvious that such a man allows himself no time or energy for constructive thought. It is not his fault, but that of those who selected him, for they have failed to recognise the qualities required for administrative responsibility. It will commonly be found that the rate of sickness absence among his staff is quite considerable, and sometimes that the administrative head is himself a sick man.

Everyone is familiar with the sense of intense frustration that follows the receipt of an adverse decision given arbitrarily, and from which there appears to be no appeal. It arouses deep emotions, often dating from the unexplained "don'ts" of early life, and the first reaction is one of anger and the desire to hit back. The administrator must be particularly on his guard in this respect, for some apparently simple action, if unexplained, may have a snowball effect in rousing latent grievances, particularly if relationships with the staff are strained and they are looking for trouble. Affronts to personal dignity seem to hurt most, and an innocent request to one person to undertake a piece of work normally performed by another may do more harm than a flat refusal to consider a promotion or an increase in salary.

Unless the habit is cultivated of considering all aspects of a problem before a decision is given, and then supporting it with reasons to the person concerned, the time will come when there will be an emotional outburst, followed by an appeal to some higher or outside authority, or, equally unfortunate, the resignation of a useful member of the organisation. The method of appeal may vary from the informal approach of the aggrieved person, or a group of the staff, to the administrator or someone senior to him, to the highly organised machinery of a trade union or national staff association. Once the wheels of the latter begin to turn they are not easy to stop, and an apparently trivial matter begins to look rather ominous when set down in black and white by an official accustomed to these matters.

This is not to say that the administrator must flinch from doing his duty as he sees it merely because some powerful organisation may make matters difficult, but rather that prevention is better than cure. It is an ancient principle of the common law that justice must be seen to be done. When an administrative act can be seen to be well-grounded and supported by good and sufficient reasons, it will stand up to the most vigorous attacks. It is the arbitrary "because I say so" type of decision that infuriates, and which will not stand the test of an appeal.

It is fortunate that the various undertakings of the present century have become so large that control no longer rests with one individual but with a group of people, for the autocrat cannot escape his human frailties, and, as Lord Acton said, "All power corrupts and absolute power corrupts absolutely". The fundamental question underlying all problems of the selection and control of staff is the purpose for which they are required. "In part it is the human problem of building up a team or series of teams of people who will work together harmoniously and in a keen spirit of co-operation." [1]

It is also necessary, however, to have regard to the nature of the tasks to be performed. Simple routine work calls for a very different type of person from that requiring original thought and creative ability. The scientist and the artist must have something of the "prima donna" in their mental and emotional make-up, and they will require much more freedom from control if they are to do good work. Similarly, they do not fit readily into large organisations unless special conditions are provided for them. This is well recognised, but it is not so readily appreciated that to-day every employee is required to have specialised knowledge of some kind. Any administrator who doubts this should try and work his own telephone switch-board for an hour or two, but, preferably, not under the eyes of those normally employed there.

[1] J. R. Simpson in G. E. Milward's *Large-Scale Organisation* published by MacDonald and Evans for the Institute of Public Administration, London, 1950, at p. 12.

Under such conditions of specialisation the old tradition of "hire and fire" of staff no longer applies. Selection calls for trained people, or those with a sufficiently high educational level as to be capable of being trained, while "control" ceases to be a disciplinary matter, but rather the adjustment of working conditions so as to provide the optimum environment for the skilled worker, with due regard to the vagaries of the human temperament.

Associated with the problem of control is that of centralisation or decentralisation. Much has been said about this, and there can be no simple answer, but no one will quarrel with the following rules outlined by Lord Heyworth, formerly Chairman of Lever Brothers and Unilever Ltd (Milward, *op. cit.*, p. 173):

"(i) The man on the spot must be either backed or removed. It is not sufficient to leave him there and confine oneself to over-ruling his decisions and recommendations.

(ii) The man on the spot is bound to make a certain number of mistakes. It is necessary, therefore, to be sparing in reproof when he exceeds his authority because initiative is a very tender plant whose growth must be fostered even if it involves a few weeds flourishing too. For the same reason care should be exercised even in criticising those decisions which he makes within his authority. It must be remembered that the function of criticism is firstly to help, and therefore we should criticise only in so far as the criticism is likely to prove helpful.

(iii) This is the most important rule. The centre must resist the temptation to add to controls. Addition can only weaken effective decentralisation."

That is, of course, particularly the point of view of the head of a great commercial undertaking, and those rules would require to be modified for such organisations as central and local government departments, where the main emphasis, apart from efficiency, is on the avoidance of mistakes and the exercise of the most rigid economy.

But the principles must remain the same. If a man or woman is to give his or her best service, as compared with the unwilling extraction of a minimum of effort, he or she must be carefully selected, trained in the work, and then trusted to get on with it. The test of good administration is the ability to get things done, and this is only possible, in the long run, when every member of the team feels that he is making a personal contribution. In order to do this he must have both the skill, ability, or aptitude for the work to be undertaken, and also the temperament which will enable him to settle comfortably into his own niche with the minimum of interference in the affairs of others.

For certain kinds of work aptitude tests to determine such matters as manual dexterity, speed and accuracy of observation, and the ability to make quick decisions, can be used. Other physical attributes, such as speed of reaction time, can also be ascertained, and a fairly accurate assessment of temperament can be made. No test, or combination of tests, can, however, take the place of the personal interview with people who know precisely what the particular work involves, the nature of the other people concerned in it, and who have the knowledge of future developments.

Rigid mechanical assessment and selection would, if carried to extremes, produce the uniformity of a row of guardsmen at a ceremonial parade. It would then be necessary to have separate selection procedures for every grade of employee, whereas, in fact, the art of selection includes the ability to spot the occasional candidate who will be prepared to accept additional responsibility in due course, when offered promotion, and who will, in his turn, choose the appropriate staff and weld them into an efficient and happy team. No amount of aptitude tests can forecast whether such a man will grow and expand with his opportunities.

CHAPTER III

THE MANAGEMENT OF AN OFFICE

The professional man or woman, when confronted with office routine for the first time, may be attracted to it, is perhaps repelled from it, or, less often, may be amused by it. The young graduate, trained to think in terms of building bridges and dams, of the economic circumstances of empires, or of the minutiae of the central nervous system, finds the details of day-to-day administration very small beer indeed. And yet it is this meticulous attention to details that will occupy much of his time, even if he ever does embark on the major projects for which he has been trained, for administration plays a more and more important part in life as one climbs the ladder of success. It is worthwhile, therefore, to pay some attention to office routine.

Fortunately, there is no deep *mystique*, and the fundamentals are quite simple. In effect, they amount to establishing a sound routine and keeping to it. Consider for a moment the hypothetical case of a young graduate, for example a mathematician, who finds himself in charge of the statistical section of a large industrial undertaking with international ramifications. When he arrives to take over his duties he discovers that he is responsible for the work of a number of other people, including statisticians, computors, and office staff, and has charge of a quantity of valuable equipment. It will be his duty to administer this unit, and also to link it effectively with the main organisation and with the outside world. The first task is clearly to become familiar with the workings of the parent body, and to find out what everybody does, or does not do. At this stage, the less he says the better.

As soon as the broad outlines of the work become clear the routine of the section can be organised and, as charity begins at home, the primary requirement is to organise one's own day so that everyone else will at least know where to find the head of the section at any given moment. There is nothing more disconcerting than to work for the brilliant but erratic administrator who can never be found when he is wanted. On the other hand, the man who arrives before everyone else, and stays long after they have gone, is equally troublesome, for he "makes" work. Incidentally, it is all too easy to make work. Unnecessary letters, reports, and telephone calls have a snowball effect, and, while the volume of

25

output may look very impressive for a time, it is not long before "that feller" becomes known and avoided.

Letters

Everyone must work according to his particular mental and physical make-up, but, in general, it is desirable to arrive at approximately the same time each day, and then to address oneself to the organisation of the day's work. It may sound trite to say that the first step is to deal with the morning's post, but it is surprising how this can be delayed if not attended to at once. It is quite unrealistic to expect typists to begin working frantically at about 4.30 p.m., quite apart from the fact that this encourages bad work, for it is then usually too late to correct mistakes.

Letter writing is an art which can be acquired only by long practice. A good secretary can do a great deal, but good secretaries are hard to come by, and the loss by marriage is heavy. Dictating machines have their advantages, but it is generally possible to detect those who use them, for they usually employ about three times the number of words required to express their meaning. For the administrator who must express himself briefly, clearly, and concisely in a letter (and who must not?), there is nothing to replace the long-hand draft. It may seem tedious, and there may be an anxious search for the right word or phrase, but the end-result justifies the effort. For long letters or a draft report, a short-hand writer or a dictating machine may ensure that the sense is committed to paper, but it is very rare indeed that these drafts can be sent out without corrections or amplifications, and they may need one or more revisions before they are fit to be despatched. It is sensible, therefore, to devote the first hour or two of the day to this work, and to send it for typing early, so that it may be returned in sufficient time to allow of adequate perusal, correction, and, if necessary, re-typing.

The next step is to go through the general work of the section or department with the secretary or chief clerk. Depending upon the volume of work, this may take only a few moments or a considerable time, for it may consist of merely a brief exchange of gossip or it may entail a detailed examination of the financial position in preparation for the annual estimates. The essential is to do it as a routine, for it leaves the rest of the morning clear for discussion with one's colleagues, for meetings, or for the work for which one has been trained.

The comment is often made that heads of departments are "snowed-under" with administration, and so they can be, but it is usually their own fault. By devoting the first hour or two regularly to routine in the manner described, it is possible to dispose of an enormous amount of paper work, and one need then return to routine only late in the afternoon, when the letters and reports come back from the typists. Here also some regularity is desirable. If it is known that letters, etc., for the evening post will be signed and ready for despatch by 5.15 p.m. each one knows where he stands. The administrative assistant who is prepared to wait about until 6.30 or 7 p.m. is very rare, and it is bad administration to expect anyone to do so, except in an emergency.

Reports

So far, these comments have been applied to routine work. There will, in addition, be lengthy reports to be read and written, visitors to be seen, and meetings to be attended. The writing of reports comes to be regarded as a most irksome task by some people. Others make light of them, and usually do them very badly. It is a good plan, when confronted with any work of this kind, to ask oneself what requires to be said. If the answer is nothing, the problem is solved. If the crux of the matter is clear, then it will almost set itself down on paper. In many instances, however, the course of events and present circumstances are obvious enough, but the conclusions and recommendations are not. There is nothing for it, in these circumstances, but to sit down and draft an essay, divided into past, present, and future.

All reports should have a clear title and an indication as to who the writer is. They should have an *Introduction*, setting down briefly what the report is about and the circumstances which have led to its being written. Then follows the *Present Position*, which contains the facts of the report; the *Discussion*, in which the subject is analysed; and, finally, the *Conclusions* and *Recommendations*.

The important thing is to get something down on paper, no matter how rough it may be to start with. No one can carry all the relevant details in his head until a satisfactory report has been formulated, so a rough draft is of great help in clarifying ideas. It is often a wise precaution to put a draft aside for a day or two and then read it again. It will now appear in much better perspective. The draft should be typed with a wide margin, and double or treble spacing between the lines to allow for additions and corrections. Insertions should be made on separate sheets of paper, and marked clearly "Insert at A on p. —". At the same time, the appropriate page should be marked "Insert A" at the precise point where these insertions should be made, for the unfortunate typists who have to make sense of drafts can work wonders, but they are not thought-readers. When all corrections have been made, the number of copies required must be clearly marked at the top of the first page, for example "Final 1 + 3" means the report is to go into final form, and that three under-copies are required in addition to the top copy. If many copies are required, they must be duplicated or an electric typewriter used, for under-copies beyond a certain number may become almost illegible with ordinary carbons.

On this question of top copies it should be remembered that important people do not like to receive carbon copies, particularly if they are bad ones. If a letter has to go out to a group of people on something that really matters, it is worth while taking the trouble to make a top copy for each person, and to sign each one personally. A letter run off on the duplicator, and signed with a rubber-stamp, often finds its level in the waste-paper basket. Beware, also, of the person who begins "Dear Sir" and ends affectionately with "yours sincerely". He has either been badly educated, or is too careless to correct his own letters. It *can* happen in any well-regulated office, but it should not occur more than once.

A detail of administration which is sometimes overlooked is to ensure that a record is kept of all letters posted, with the date and the name and address of the recipient. A postage book serves a double purpose. It is a permanent record that something has, in fact, been sent, and it is a check on the costs of postage, which can be produced to the auditors when required.

Reference has been made to visitors to be seen and meetings to be attended. Here the question of an adequate appointments system arises, for there is nothing more irksome for either party than a last-minute cancellation or a forgotten appointment. A good secretary can do much, but nothing can absolve the administrator from failing to look at his diary, preferably at the end of each week and noting the events for the ensuing week. This has the added merit of giving time to think about any meeting or visit that is likely to be difficult or unusual. Visitors, especially, are not lightly to be turned away, for they represent contacts with the outside world which can be most valuable.

Meetings fall into various categories. Some *must* be attended. Others, not so important, may be worth attending if one has nothing better to do. There is a certain type of man who finds it extremely difficult to say no to any invitation, and who may, indeed, come to regard any meeting as incomplete without his presence. Sooner or later, however, there comes a time when one must be selective, and it is advisable to cultivate the habit of making well in advance a courteous apology for absence. This helps those who arrange the meetings, especially if a quorum is required.

The telephone is a most useful instrument, but it can also be a great time-waster, and it may be necessary to install some form of interception, whereby incoming calls are taken, in the first place, by another person. Various devices are available for this purpose, but the principal danger is that if they are used too frequently the individual concerned may become so elusive as to be considered not worthy of the effort of pursuit.

An irritating defect of the human mind is its ability to forget essential details at a critical moment. Because of this it is advisable to have a scribbling block on the desk on which any salient points can be noted. It is particularly necessary for important telephone conversations, both as headings for the speaker so that he remembers what to say, and as an *aide-memoire*. Important, as well as unpleasant conversations, whether by telephone or interview, should be recorded, and the note kept in a confidential file, and so also should any records which may relate to official or legal action.

Mention has been made of the value of a good secretary. The operative word is, of course, "good", for an inefficient secretary is worse than useless. A policy which experience has shown to be effective is to recruit a junior straight from school at the age of fifteen or sixteen, after careful enquiry of the headmistress as to the girl's general ability and steadiness, and put her in charge of the telephone switchboard and enquiry desk. The Post Office is most helpful in arranging for a telephone supervisor to train such a girl, and it is remarkable how quickly, within a week or two, she becomes efficient at the switchboard. The next step is to place a typewriter in front of her, with a request to type envelopes and the like. If she displays interest and aptitude, then she should be encouraged to take a shorthand and typing course, for example at the local technical college. By this means a steady flow of competent typists, who know the routine of the section, office, or department, is assured, and, more important still, whose loyalty is unquestioned. Once in a while a girl appears who is much above the average in intelligence, aptitude, and powers of concentration. Such a one should be given gradually increasing amounts of responsibility by being assigned from time to time to special duties such as filing, simple accounts, or technical responsibilities.

It is a mistake to imagine that all women, or men for that matter, are thirsting for increased responsibility. Many are not, and they are quite content with a routine job which leaves their minds free to wander or remain blank, and which conserves their energies for their pastimes. It is fortunate that this is so, for these people cheerfully undertake the drudgery, such as the routine copy-typing and similar uninteresting jobs.

It is also a myth that all that matters is the size of the weekly pay packet, for good working conditions and congenial work are valued very highly. If that were not so then no one would ever work for a university. It is worth while paying great attention to the working conditions of the staff, and especially to the layout of working rooms, with particular reference to adequate space, a modicum of privacy, and bright and cheerful decorations. Adequate lighting, both general and at the point of work, is essential, but glare should be eliminated by curtains or venetian blinds, or both. The modern fabrics and plastics have made office furnishings of this kind both cheap and effective. Particular attention should be paid to typing and other desks for special manipulative activities, so that the hands and arms are used in a natural position and not held artificially high.

Another matter worthy of careful thought, particularly in a small office, is the arrangements to be made for the welfare and relaxation of the staff. Senior officers may pretend to become so absorbed in their work as to ignore the need for breaks of any kind, but people engaged in repetitive work, such as typists and computors, or clerical officers on routine duties, must have somewhere to meet and talk over the mid-morning coffee or a cup of tea in the afternoon. It need not be elaborately furnished so long as it is recognised as being for the staff. Any tendency to linger can be checked discreetly, but, in fact, the need to do so seldom, if ever, arises. When it does, or when discord is evident from other sources, it is usually due to one of two causes: an unhappy office due to the faults of the man at the top, or a trouble-maker among the staff.

Painful though it may be, a little introspection is profitable on these occasions, for it often happens that the senior man, or his deputy, is at loggerheads with himself and needs a brief holiday. The driver, who has quickened the pace too much, may see the results in the strained faces and irritable moods of his staff, and, if he persists, in the rising sickness absence rate. The slack senior, or the absentee, cannot complain if his organisation takes the pace from him. Of the two, the driver is to be preferred, for everyone likes to be busy, but a sudden rush of work looks mountainous to those who are unaccustomed to it. It is, of course, the steady flow that achieves most, but this is not always possible, particularly in research units.

The Trouble-Maker

The trouble-maker is a difficult problem, particularly if he or she has security of tenure and cannot be dismissed. The frontal attack is usually the best, but it should only be made after careful thought and preparation, and on unassailable grounds. There must be no question of threats or bluff, for once these have proved to be ineffective the battle is lost. Above all, the person conducting the interview must keep his temper, although he may allow himself to appear to lose it.

Much depends on the temperament of the trouble-maker. If he is a psychopath, and many are, martyrdom may be welcome, and a first-class row is a tonic to such a person. The direct approach may then only aggravate matters. It may be possible to put the difficult one on work where he is kept to himself. Incidentally, people of this kind are sometimes above the average in intelligence, and respond to being given difficult tasks. Others are sub-normal, and subside quietly when given something simple and routine in nature. It is worth while, therefore, exploring the possibility of giving employment elsewhere in the organisation. A method which is not to be commended, but which is sometimes adopted in large organisations, is to recommend such an individual strongly for promotion in the hope that he will be transferred to another section. Indeed, a senior official in one large service used to boast, many years ago, that he had arrived at his present position by being "kicked upstairs" every time he made himself awkward!

The amount of friction which can be generated in a small office by a trouble-maker is very considerable, and the head of the section, department, or office concerned then has a most difficult task in deciding when to intervene and when to turn a "blind eye". In general, it is desirable to interfere as little as possible, for premature intervention in a local quarrel may turn it into a major issue, with a staff united against interference in their affairs. On the other hand, delay until the matter reaches the stage of resignations of competent officers is merely weakness, and the plea of ignorance is no excuse, for it is the administrator's job to know what is going on, or to sense that all is not well. As in all these matters, intervention, when it comes, must be decisive. A firm ruling, even if it is wrong, is much to be preferred to a feeble gesture, and there is no doubt that people respect a certain amount of authoritarianism. Incidentally, a firm hand is usually the best way of dealing with the psychopath, who may be merely bolstering his own sense of insecurity. If "authority" decides, then his personal doubts are resolved for him.

Filing

A problem in all organisations, but especially in the small ones, is the filing system. The ideal of any method is simple. It is merely that papers and correspondence shall be stored in such an orderly fashion that they can be found at a moment's notice. In order to effect this, more and more elaborate systems may be devised, until eventually the stage is reached of a separate registry, with trained staff, card indexes, photographic apparatus, printed and labelled files, special messengers, and so on.

The simplest system is, of course, a filing cabinet with the subjects arranged in alphabetical order, but the novice is at once faced with the problem of what to file and under which heading. Is everything to go in, or are some things to be retained for current action? *Chacun à son goût*, but a sensible working arrangement is to keep urgent matters on the desk until settled, and confidential and personal matters in a locked cabinet in one's own room.

The "in", "out", and "pending" trays on a government official's table are not there for fun. A Civil Service file contains every available scrap of information on the subject under consideration, and no central government administrator would dream of answering any enquiry until he had sent for the appropriate file, and looked carefully through it. If the question before him is a technical one, he will "minute" the file to one of his expert colleagues for advice. If a policy decision is required at a higher level, he will gather the threads together in a note for his superiors. The file then travels to them. Only by this means can the central government machine be made to work efficiently. It may appear to be cumbersome and slow, but it ensures that every aspect of the matter is considered before a reply is sent. Incidentally, the efficiency of the machine cannot be judged from the cautious nature of the final reply, for it must be remembered that the first duty of the civil servant is to safeguard the minister at the head of his department. Consideration of what it is expedient to say plays a large part in the public service.

This elaborate organisation is not required in a small office, but the principles are similar. No letter should be answered without a glance through the previous correspondence, and matters on which action is current should be kept conveniently to hand in a "pending" tray. When they have been completed, the papers are transferred to the "out" tray for postage and filing. It goes without saying that a copy should be kept of all correspondence and reports. Personal matters should be kept separate in a "personal" file, and confidential matters, especially those likely to lead to litigation, should also be kept separately.

It is a good plan to maintain a separate record, on cards or in a file kept in a private locked cabinet, for each member of the staff. This should be retained after the individual leaves, for it is valuable in drafting testimonials or references, and it is amusing to see how thick the files of the "difficult" people become. One man experienced in selecting candidates was asked the secret of his success. He said: "Well, I pick up the dossiers before me and weigh them in my hand. The lightest one wins".

When pending, personal, and confidential papers have been dealt with there remains the problem of filing of general papers, and here it is tempting to paraphrase Pope and say that "Whate'er is filed best is best". In fact, it is the person who does the filing who counts most, and it is worth selecting one member of the staff to be responsible for filing duties, preferably part-time, for it is a dull job. Some secretaries like to do their own filing, but this often means that a mountain of papers accumulates in the corner of the room, and sooner or later someone who happens to be slack is pressed into service to "help". This is usually disastrous, for it results merely in a mechanical selection of *A*, *B*, or *C*, regardless of content or sense, and one day the whole office will find itself engaged on a special search for missing papers. There are plenty of good filing systems if only they are used intelligently.

As time goes on the decision must be made as to how long papers should be kept. Much depends on the nature of the office. Government and legal documents may need to be kept indefinitely. Hospital and medical records must be retained for a minimum of six years, and are usually kept for a much longer time than this. Routine business papers, receipts for payment and the like, can be destroyed at the end of one or two years, but it may be desirable to retain receipts for expensive or special items of equipment for a longer time as they may be useful in any claim for insurance.

A matter which is often neglected, but which is part of the responsibility of anyone in administrative charge, is to make sure, periodically, that there is no risk of fire, and that the arrangements to meet an outbreak are in good order. It is really quite remarkable what the best-intentioned members of the staff can do. Ventilators become stuffed up with paper or cloths in cold weather. Empty corners and shelves become cluttered up with boxes, and personal possessions are left in odd places. Anyone who takes a pride in his organisation should do a complete inspection at least once a year. The inspection should be literally into every nook and cranny, preferably notebook in hand. Any defects found should be remedied at once, rubbish removed, and fire and welfare precautions attended to. Each first-aid box should be opened and

the contents checked, and renewed where necessary. Opportunity
should also be taken to review the state of repair and decoration
of the building, and to make arrangements for renovations.

These visits of inspection serve a number of purposes. They
are a useful education to the administrative head of the office,
they show the staff that there is such a person and that he is
apparently a human being, and they give an opportunity to meet
people, such as the telephonist and the stoker-handyman, on their
own ground. A word of praise for a well-kept boiler-room is
worth a great deal to the man who works there.

Finance

A subject which causes much anxiety to the administrator who
finds himself in charge of an office for the first time is the financial
aspect of the work. It is inadvisable to rely too much on the
secretary, for there will come a day of reckoning when she is not
there, and her system, which worked well with her, may be quite
incomprehensible to anyone else. Secretaries often develop queer
short-cuts of their own, and a kind of sign language which only
they can understand. The first question is how much money is
available and for what period. Most departments work on an
annual basis, and the records of expenditure for the current year
are a valuable guide for the preparation of estimates for the next.

Without becoming too technical, it must be noted that expenditure falls into two divisions. There is the initial outlay to build
or purchase a thing, known as capital or non-recurrent expenditure,
and there is the money required to keep it running, recurrent
expenditure. It is essential not to embark on a project, or to buy
expensive apparatus, without making sure that enough money is
available to maintain it, and money in this connection may mean
wages for staff. Elaborate computing apparatus, for example, may
be most efficient and time-saving, provided that it is properly and
regularly maintained and with adequate staff to work it. Many
people tend to think only in terms of capital expenditure and to
forget the subsequent costs.

Given an adequate building, staff, and equipment, the immediate
problem is to keep it going efficiently and economically. Here a
regular routine is essential. Bills must be scrutinised and paid
regularly, preferably on a monthly or quarterly basis, and properly
entered in the books. A petty cash account is essential for small
day-to-day purposes, but items must be booked at once, and anyone who "raids" the petty cash must leave a note to that effect.
Irregular incursions into the petty cash are not to be encouraged,
for they always lead to trouble sooner or later. One responsible

person should be in charge, and it should be kept in a locked cash-box in the safe. A safe is a good investment, even if second-hand. It will not necessarily stop the professional thief, but it puts tempta-tion out of the way of everyone else.

Where accounts are run on a monthly or quarterly basis it is advisable to draw up a comprehensive statement at the same time, showing the total expenditure to date under the various headings as compared with the estimates, and also the amount of money available for the rest of the year.

Any deficit should be shown in red, so that it can be seen immediately. By this means the progress of expenditure can be kept regularly under supervision, and sudden panic averted. Such a routine also allows for proper consideration of any heavy item of expenditure in relation to the requirements of the department as a whole.

It is perhaps unnecessary to emphasise that all bills, whether from nationalised industries, or from the little shop round the corner, should be examined before being passed for payment. Deliberate fraud or excessive charging is rare, but mistakes are quite common, particularly in the submitting of the same account twice. In large industries the machinery for sending out accounts is sometimes kept separate from the receiving office, and delay occurs before payment is notified from one to the other. In this context it should be noted that computers must depend on the accuracy of those who feed them and they may also make mistakes.

Before ordering an expensive or unusual item it is advisable to secure estimates from several different firms, and if a higher price than is usual is paid a note should be kept of the reason, for example that facilities for servicing are more readily available. Then, if the item is subsequently questioned by the auditors, a reasonable explanation is immediately forthcoming. Many firms are prepared to arrange discount for a regular customer, and this is particularly useful for such items as printing and stationery.

Annual Estimates

Preparation of annual estimates can be a rather alarming experi-ence for the newcomer. The basic principles are quite simple, neither to over-estimate nor to under-estimate. Over-estimation of expenditure, if persisted in, will soon become apparent, and will lead, sooner or later, to heavy pruning of the estimates by the parent organisation. Under-estimation is equally dangerous, for it is likely to lead to a deficit at the end of the year. A safe plan is to base the estimates on the experience of the previous year, or better still the previous three or four years, cutting down where the headings show a considerable excess of income over expenditure, keeping level where conditions are clearly static, but watching warily the items which have always been near the border-line, or where national trends indicate the likelihood of a rise in prices. Thus, fuel is a heavy item in any estimates, even if bought at the cheaper rates applying during the summer. If the estimate, say for coke, has been of the order of £180 for the past two years, but increased transport charges are pending, then it would be reasonable to increase the estimate to £200. A margin or reserve must be kept for unexpected items, and a figure of 10 per cent. would not be unreasonable for this. It need not necessarily appear as a separate item, but may be divided among the various headings that comprise the estimate.

The foregoing comments relate, of course, to current expenditure. Non-recurrent expenditure is dealt with separately, or in a separate part of the estimates. Here, it is advisable to ask all senior members of the staff well in advance what their requirements are likely to be, and, if necessary, to call a meeting to discuss them, for it will not be possible to satisfy everyone. Arbitrary decisions by the head of the department can be most disheartening to someone who badly needs a piece of apparatus, whereas if it can be demonstrated that the cake, such as it is, has been evenly divided, or that one person is given a larger slice because the others think he should have it, there will be little occasion for grumbles.

The newcomer to administration, acutely conscious of his own defects, tends to regard any setback to his plans as a kind of personal insult. If he is not very careful he will fix all the blame on "them", for "they" are obstructing him in his progress. For example, a letter, perhaps not too tactfully worded, may arrive saying curtly that such and such an item of expenditure has not been approved. The natural reaction is to reply angrily and immediately, and emotion usually lends a cutting edge to one's powers of expression. The writer of the first letter therefore receives a rude jolt by return of post, and is placed automatically on the defensive. A succession of rather acid missives then ensues, in which the more experienced man wins, especially if he holds the purse-strings.

Ideally, no letter should be written in anger, but delayed for twenty-four hours. It is quite surprising what a clarifying effect a night's rest can have. If the grievance remains the next day a more reasoned reply can be made, explaining in detail why the request was made, and asking for an explanation for the refusal to authorise it. As "they" are usually ordinary, sometimes very ordinary, people, a better course is to telephone or see the

writer of the letter before spilling any ink. If correspondence is
unavoidable, letters should be so worded that they cannot have a
boomerang effect. There is nothing more disconcerting than to be
confronted with one's earlier and contradictory statements. If it
seems likely that the matter may have to be referred to some
higher authority, such as a Finance and General Purposes Committee, care should be taken to use temperate language, and to
avoid any appearance of usurping the authority of the committee.
Dictators are not popular at any level of society, and to acquire
early in one's career the reputation for being unduly aggressive
can be a great handicap.

Apart from this, there are usually good reasons behind any
action on "their" part, although these may not be apparent. It
may, for example, seem eminently reasonable to the head of a
small section of a large organisation that someone in his office
who has done good work should have special recognition. The
weary and disillusioned central administrator, however, may know
perfectly well that fifty other heads of sections have put in similar
claims, and the structure of the organisation may be such that the
proposal is impracticable anyway.

The essential thing to remember is that "they" are not inspired
by malice. They may be ignorant of technical work, or tired, or
bored, and, at worst, they may not be interested in anything except
keeping the wheels turning, but they are never collectively vindic-
tive, and they are usually open to reason within the framework of
their powers.

It is a far cry from the administration of a small department
or office, as described in this chapter, to vast organisations, such
as the Pentagon in Washington, with its own internal post office
and a shopping centre catering for 30,000 workers,[1] but the ele-
mentary principles remain the same. Mechanisation may enable
many routine procedures to be done by one girl after a brief
training, documents can be copied in a moment, or transmitted
round the world by teleprinter. The administrator can communicate, if he wishes, with his colleagues on the other side of the
world by radio messages bounced off the moon. Alternatively,
he may travel to them at the speed of sound.

All these aids to administration are so impressive that they
tend to obscure the fundamentals. If the girl tending the machine
is not properly selected and trained, or if her health, comfort, and
welfare, are not supervised, she will make mistakes. In a small

[1] E. N. Gladden, *The Essentials of Public Administration*, Staples Press
1964, p. 43.

organisation a mistake soon becomes obvious, and is quickly recti-
fied. In a machine capable of multiplying by millions, one small
error may be very costly indeed.

Similarly, the incompetent administrator remains incompetent
no matter how big the electronic computers are in his organisation,
for no machine has yet been devised which can make a "human"
decision. There is, alas, no room for the lovable Dickensian
eccentric in the corner of a dark and stuffy office, who retained
his place because of his encyclopaedic knowledge. Nor can the
"senior partner" now make a few arbitrary decisions before retiring
to his club. It was characteristic of those individualists, however,
that they understood human nature, and the first requirement of
any successful administrator is that he must have a knowledge of
the strengths and weaknesses of the people he deals with. This is
best acquired in a small office.

It is often said that a fundamental requirement for successful
administration is organising ability "of the highest order", as if
this were a gift possessed by some but not by others. While it is
true that some individuals are endowed with a quickness of per-
ception and an agility of mind which makes it easy for them to
grasp the essentials of a problem, the fact remains that it is intense
application, the "infinite capacity for taking pains", allied to
staying power over long periods of time, that makes for good
organising ability. Courage and intuition are not enough. If they
were it would not have been necessary for Sir Vivian Fuchs to
spend so long in organising his journey across Antarctica.

Firmness and flexibility sound an odd combination of qualities,
but they are both required. The courage to adhere to an unpopular
course or decision, if it is the right one, must be allied with the
ability to adapt quickly to a changed set of circumstances. Perhaps the most cherished virtue of the competent administrator, and
one which can continually be cultivated, is self-control, for without
this it would be impossible to co-ordinate the activities of the
team on whose efforts success in any enterprise depends. The
wayward, eccentric, genius has no place in the modern administrative framework except, perhaps, as an adviser in some special
subject. It is in the steady application of a soundly constructed,
intelligent, and contented team that the secret of success lies. The
management of such a team is an acquired art, which can only be
practised adequately if the administrative structure, the organisation, is designed for the purpose.

CHAPTER IV

THE SPECIALIST AND THE GENERAL ADMINISTRATOR

In the sixteenth Haldane Memorial Lecture, given by Sir John Anderson (later Lord Waverley) in 1949, he said: "Only a few years ago it would not have been difficult to find a man of experience ready to deny the very existence of such a thing as an art of administration".[1]   He was comparing conditions as they were when he first entered the Civil Service in 1905, when the functions of public officials were regulative rather than executive, with the developments in the study of organisation and methods some forty-five years later.

Within the span of the present century there has developed not only the art of administration, but also the general administrator. There has also been the most remarkable extension of specialist knowledge, with the employment of medical men, engineers, architects, lawyers, and other professional people in central and local government services, and in industry.

This expansion has taken place without any corresponding definition of the powers and duties of the specialist and the general administrator.   The former has usually had only a scientific or technical training, and, with the notable exception of the lawyer, has seldom had contact, even in theory, with the administrative machine.   The lawyer, by reason of his studies in legal history and constitutional law, and in contract and tort, is much more clearly aware of the intricacies of government and management, and the "learned clerk", the administrator of former times, was almost always a lawyer by training.

Although the need for the trained administrator is now clearly recognised, the form his training takes varies greatly, and there is still a large element of "learning on the job".   That, in itself, is all to the good, but it means that each general administrator must acquire by experience, as a matter of trial and error, the knowledge of how to deal with his specialist colleagues, and how far he may intervene in their affairs without appearing to interfere.

Precedents are of little value to him.   The political struggles in the latter half of the last century were of a specialised kind,

[1] *Administrative Technique in the Public Services.*   16th Haldane Memorial Lecture, 1949, Sir John Anderson, published by the University of London.

with the clash of personalities playing a considerable part. In any event, there was then no question, as there is to-day, of whole professions becoming involved by a process of nationalisation, or by the growth of great industries on a national or international scale. The position is now vastly different, for, as Lewis and Maude said in *Professional People*, in 1952: "It is clear that one of the immediate challenges which faces the professions is that of administration; and closely bound up with administration is leadership".[1]

Sometimes there is no problem. The expert is employed as an adviser or consultant, and the clerk or secretary transmits this advice to the executive or policy-making body. The latter is free to accept or reject the advice tendered, or to ask for further information. The trouble begins when positive action is required, either technical or administrative. Assume, for a moment, that the executive body decides to build something, a hospital, or a bridge, or a factory. Very early in the proceedings the general administrator may find that he requires the help of experts, for example of lawyers to complete the purchase of land, of architects to design the building, or of engineers or surveyors as the case may be. As soon as any one of these specialists accepts personal responsibility he becomes a part of the administrative structure, and ceases to be merely a passive adviser. The position then becomes not unlike that of a chief engineer in a ship. The captain must give orders to direct the vessel safely on its course, but as soon as a problem occurs in the engine-room he is powerless, for no amount of orders from the bridge will repair a broken propeller shaft. This is perhaps the first and hardest lesson for the general administrator to learn, namely, that he neglects expert advice at his peril. If professional advice is tendered to the effect that something or other will not work it may prove to be wrong, but to ignore it would be to gamble against heavy odds, and no layman in his senses would do so. Almost equally disastrous would be the failure to seek expert advice in case it should prove to be unpalatable.

So far, however, we are still on fairly safe ground. The administrator is within his province, and the only complaint of the specialist can be that he was not consulted, or that his advice was ignored. Let us go one stage further. The preliminary formalities have been completed, decisions on policy have been made, and the land acquired. Now begins the task of building or creating something on it. Again the position may be relatively

---

[1] *Professional People*, Lewis, E. M. R., and Maude, A. E., Phoenix House Ltd, London, 1952, at p. 270.

simple. A private firm of consulting architects or engineers may be employed for this particular work, under a contract drawn up by independent lawyers or by the administrator if he is himself a lawyer. The administrator has merely delegated responsibility to them, and he is still in an impeccable position. Where, however, the constructive work is transferred to professional officers within the same employment the position can become very difficult indeed, particularly if the general administrator insists on keeping a tight hold on the reins. It could be argued that all he has to do is to hand over responsibility, both administrative and technical, but a moment's thought will show that this is impossible, for it would mean that each successive group of experts would take charge for a time, or that one of these would himself have to assume the function of general administrator. Quite apart from the fact that experts are notoriously lacking in administrative skill, the whole essence of administration, indeed the *raison d'être* of the general administrator, is the smooth co-ordination of an enterprise.

So far, so good; the administrator's task is to knit together all loose ends and to make for smooth working by the experts. Why, then, all the talk about "danger" to the professions and the need for "leadership"? The danger arises partly from the fact that some administrators have never done anything but sit in an office. Their experience of human frailties and weaknesses is thus limited, and their knowledge of practical difficulties in the field may be negligible. They are, therefore, doubly handicapped when confronted with the "prima donnas", for they do not understand the stresses to which these people are subjected by their work or their reactions to them nor can they comprehend that paper plans, specifications, and time-tables are liable to modifications when they come to be put into practice.

This is particularly well shown in law and medicine. The architect and the engineer can demand that the materials with which they work must reach a certain standard of quality. They can, within certain limits, forecast the stresses and strains that the structures they are creating will have to bear. The lawyer, on the other hand, can never be quite certain that an individual case will stand the test of an action in the courts, and he safeguards his position with what may appear to be excessive caution. The doctor is dealing with the most plastic and frail material of all. It is not without justification that medicine is still regarded as an art rather than a science. Precise knowledge of human anatomy, physiology, biochemistry, and pathology do not enable even the most experienced man to predict how the individual patient before him will respond, and success in clinical medicine, as in the practice of law, remains very much a matter of individual judgment.

As mentioned above, the "danger" arises only partly from the limited horizon of some administrators. It is equally true to say that many professional men have no idea whatever of administration. Even the composition of a letter may be a major effort, except on their own subject, and the training of the scientist leaves little time or inclination for the niceties of the English, or indeed any other, language. The result is often a sense of frustration and rage when confronted with an administrator who only too clearly knows all the answers on paper, but who is out of touch and out of sympathy with the practical difficulties likely to be encountered.

These differences would be of relatively little moment if they were restricted to a small office or department, for they would then be of no more importance than many other possible causes of friction between individuals. It is a characteristic of the twentieth century, however, that increasing numbers of professional men are becoming concerned with administration, and caught up in the administrative machine. By a curious twist of fate they are, in many instances, having to create their own administrative organisations, in the form of professional associations and negotiating bodies, and to employ professional administrators to look after their interests.

It is no longer a question of the individual administrator and the professional man, but of administrative and technical divisions and departments, with separate floors and sometimes whole buildings allocated to each. Detailed administrative control on the one hand, and purely professional advice on the other, then become almost impossible. The administrator must either create an administrative ring in the professional divisions, or the professional man must turn administrator. It is now acknowledged that senior posts in all professional services carry increasing administrative responsibility. Within the universities, for example, this is recognised by additional payment to heads of departments for administrative duties.

It is a logical development. Take, for example, the architectural division of a large service. Only the chief architect can say what the special requirements of his staff are and what their working conditions should be, and he must relate these to the overall policy and financial budget as defined by the general administrators. The latter, for their part, will leave the day-to-day administration to him, and carry out their proper function of co-ordination in the interests of the efficiency of the organisation as a whole.

Unfortunately, this ideal state of affairs is not always attainable. Sometimes the administrator is not big enough for the job, and is happiest when prying into tiny items of expenditure or insisting on strict observance of some rule, as he did when he was young. The professional man may be equally incompetent, with no administrative sense whatever, or, even worse, a kind of "sea lawyer", who thinks that he knows better than the trained general administrator. Everyone is familiar with the type of man whose first instinct is to reach for the Statutes and Ordinances, or some similar book, and who is an authority on precedents which prove why a thing should not be done.

Examples of this kind may always be found, but they do not affect the main issue. Where the organisation has become so complicated that the work has to be sectionalised, the head of each section must be left to administer it. If he is not competent to do so he must be replaced. The function of the general administrator then becomes one of general supervision and co-ordination. He is, in effect, *primus inter pares*, and the greatest care must be exercised to ensure that this position is clearly maintained. Relevant information must be passed on at once, and the appropriate professional chiefs consulted on all occasions. They, in their turn, must not shirk responsibility for their actions and for those of their staffs. There can be no question of insisting on the formalities of responsibility without shouldering the burdens also.

It is now possible to see why Lewis and Maude (*vide supra*) linked administration with leadership, for a leader is one who shows the way, and anyone who accepts administrative responsibility must clearly know how to administer, and be able to show others how to do so. The time is long past when the professional man could "leave all that to the clerks", for the professions themselves have become, in a sense, administrative units in the conduct both of their internal and of their external affairs. This process is, as yet, far from complete, and it explains some of the difficulties. In general, the ancient and learned professions, such as the Church, law, and medicine, are at a disadvantage as compared with those which have matured more recently, for these old callings were concerned particularly with their internal affairs. Their organisations were designed to further professional knowledge, and to maintain a high standard of integrity, with the supervision of education and discipline vested within the profession.

It is obvious that this type of organisation does not lend itself readily to the negotiating machinery required when its members become servants of the State, or employees of a large industrial concern. Traditionally independent, and intense individualists in their work, professional men do not take kindly to collective bargaining, and when they undertake it their high standard of ethics and their inexperience may make them easy victims for a time. The initial naïve and trusting period is often succeeded by one of cynical disillusionment, due to misunderstanding on both sides, and it is not until they evolve their own skilled administrators that equilibrium is reached. By that time, however, much of the goodwill may have evaporated.

The more recently developed professions, such as the architects and engineers, are better placed, partly by reason of their training, which now includes a considerable amount of business administration and instruction in human relations in industry, and partly because their work brings them directly into contact with large-scale enterprise, so that they are familiar with the methods employed. The successful architect or engineer must, of necessity, develop a strong administrative sense.

It is not always easy to say what constitutes a "professional" person, for new professions arise, and clamour for recognition through their organisations. When these become numerous the central administration may attempt to group them together, and try to negotiate terms and conditions of service on a broad basis. The results may be sometimes rather odd. Ancillary or para-medical workers, for example, may include medico-social workers, health-visitors, and chiropodists, to say nothing of physiotherapists, occupational therapists, and psychiatric social workers. Such a mixed bag makes for administrative headaches, but it must be sorted out patiently if the optimum working conditions are to be obtained. It might be said, for example, that doctors and dentists are comparable, in that they both deal with human tissues, but, in fact, their working conditions are quite different.

The criticism is sometimes made that administrators tend to breed administrators, and that administrative costs are unduly heavy. While it is true that inefficient administration is costly, the reverse applies to a competent organisation, for it ensures that the specialist is freed from worrying details and enabled to make the best use of his expert knowledge.

It is also said, on occasion, that the general administrator can do all that is necessary, and that the professional man need not trouble to acquire this expertise. If carried too far that doctrine could result in the specialist being down-graded to the status of a technician merely applying some special skill at the request of another. Such a development would be harmful to everyone, and not least to the general administrator, for the creative and artistic side of the specialist would become dormant, and original thought would be stifled. Apart from this the skilled specialist administrator can be of great value to the general administrator, for he then speaks, as it were, both languages. Any risk that the two interests may clash is a calculated one and worth taking. It can be minimised by seeing that the general principles of administration are properly taught and fully understood on both sides.

The understanding has been implicit throughout this brief review that the art of administration, in its twentieth-century setting, is only in its infancy. Even the administrative tools are changing rapidly with the development of electronic computers, the instantaneous copying of documents, new filing systems, and a host of other devices. One fact is quite clear. The administrative dictator and the "Pooh-bah" are anachronisms. Any clerk to a local authority, for instance, who attempted to arrogate all administrative power to himself, if such a foolish man could be found, would speedily find himself superannuated. It has become physically impossible for one man to control a modern organisation single-handed for any length of time, and the sickness and mortality rates of administrators in certain new services built on the old administrative patterns have been very high indeed.

No one can forsee the final form of administration, if, indeed, there can be such a thing. In the meantime, it will suffice to pick good men, to train them well, and then to leave them to get on with their work, whether this be general or specialised. The development of administrative and staff training institutions, for both general and specialised forms of administration, is one of the major developments of recent years and augurs well for the future.

CHAPTER V

ORGANISATION AND MANAGEMENT

A feature of modern times, and especially of the present century, has been the increasing awareness that management, whether of public or private business, is a subject requiring specialised knowledge and training. It is not so much a question of the emergence of a separate managerial class of men and women, as of ensuring that a nation dependent on industrial efficiency for survival should be fully equipped with the most modern methods in a highly competitive world.

In preceding chapters the art of administration was discussed. It is now necessary to consider the people who operate the administrative machine and make it "tick", and the conditions under which they work. There are many aspects to this problem, including the interplay of personalities summed up in the term "human relations".

The techniques of planning and of translating plans into practical and productive effort, communications, the design and maintenance of offices and other work places, and, above all, the study of efficiency with due regard to human dignity, must also be considered. There has been much talk of "fitting the job to the man" instead of fitting the man to the job, but the truth lies in matching the two, for excessive consideration for the welfare and comfort of the individual could result in making the work that he does unproductive and so putting him out of a job entirely.

This subject is now beginning to receive attention in many fields. Some universities, notably in the United States of America, have separate schools of business and administration, others have professorships in accountancy and related subjects. Some universities run special post-graduate courses, in association with industry, for the training of managers, while others include business administration within their undergraduate syllabus. Many of the large industries, notably those with wide ramifications overseas, organise training courses for their own employees, and so also do some employers' associations and trade unions.

Just as it has proved necessary to engage professional auditors to examine financial accounts, so it is becoming evident that a regular audit of efficiency is necessary if the machine is to be kept up to date and in good order. The scope of the word "audit" is, therefore, changing. Formerly it was accepted as implying an examination of the financial accounts in order to establish the state of solvency of the undertaking, and the probity of those engaged in it. Now it is recognised that auditing has become an instrument of efficient organisation and management, dealing not only with finance, but also with the administrative system, which may have wide ramifications.

It is perhaps advisable at this stage to look again at the origins of the modern administrative system, for they are quite simple. Early in the history of any undertaking, whether it be public or private, two requirements may be seen. First, there is the need for written records. The clerk or scribe, therefore, required one qualification, the ability to read and write, and his attainments in this respect were not rated very highly. He was, in fact, a humble but necessary officer. The other essential was for some trustworthy person to receive and disburse monies—the bursar, or keeper of the purse.

Similarly, the medieval merchant was self-contained, with his pen and ink-horn, and perhaps a boy to act as personal assistant. Even up to the early part of the present century, the organisation of many offices was simple. The "boss" remained personally responsible, a clerk with a natural aptitude for figures kept the accounts, while another supervised the general running of the office with some such title as chief or managing clerk.

Much the same pattern could be seen in the local authorities. The clerk, usually a lawyer in the large authorities, but often with no special training in the smaller, might be full-time or part-time, and the business of the council was conducted on a personal basis, with chairman and members "dropping in" to his office, or meeting him over luncheon at the local club, a pattern familiar to many within living memory. The clerk to a major authority might hold a number of public offices, especially if he were a lawyer of some standing. The keeping of accounts was, in general, a matter of relatively minor importance, to be delegated to officials who had perhaps served their apprenticeship in the office of the poor law relieving officer, or of the master of the local workhouse.

The development of experts in all these fields is largely a product of the present century, and the centralisation of power in the hands of one or two people, which formed the essence of success in more leisurely times, has become rare. Instead, the professional administrator has appeared in all fields of activity, and it is by his strengths or weaknesses that the efforts of the present century will be judged. If the administrative machine is kept flexible and maintained intelligently it will be efficient. If it becomes clogged with petty restrictions, rules, and regulations, so that those who tend it have no time to consider the effectiveness of their work, it will fail.

So important has this problem become that it has received consideration from many bodies since Lord Chief Justice Hewart first drew attention to the dangers of bureaucracy in *New Despotism* in 1929.

Here it becomes necessary to look again at terminology. What is the difference, for example, between the "administrator" and the "admin. block" in a public service and the "manager" and the "manager's office" in a private undertaking? The word *administrator* has acquired a certain cloak of respectability, but if good management is the art of getting something done quickly, economically, and efficiently, then all administrators are, or should be, managers. It is this faculty of enabling "ordinary people to do the work of superior people", a saying attributed to Rockefeller, that comprises the art of management, and it is in this sense that it is used in this chapter.

The term *organisation* presents less difficulty, for it is generally accepted to mean the structure of an undertaking, the anatomy, so to speak, without which it would be impossible for it to function at all. To take an analogy from the human body, the most perfectly developed and educated cerebral cortex would be quite useless without paths of communication with the rest of the body, supplies of oxygen and nutrition through the respiratory and digestive systems, and the removal of waste products by the excretory organs. Even that is not enough, for there must also be an efficient locomotor system of muscles and joints to enable purposive action to be taken.

Similarly, with the pattern of organisation there are certain essential requirements. First and foremost, there must be a definite plan or policy, an aim or goal. In order that this may be defined clearly, and the route towards the objective mapped out, all relevant facts must be known and they must be accurate. The question, "What is the purpose of the exercise?", is a most valuable one, and should be asked frequently. When the basic facts have been checked and accepted, and policy defined, there must be a motive force to induce, or spur on, action. That force may be altruism, for example, compassion for the sufferings of others, which forms so important an element of the great religious movements of the world. On the other hand, the main source of stimulation may be fear, for instance the epidemics of cholera in Europe a little over 100 years ago, which led to many improvements in the public services. But perhaps the greatest spur of all is economic necessity. The imperative need to preserve the health of skilled craftsmen, and to prolong their working lives if possible, began to appear with the growth of industrialisation in western Europe, and that process is still continuing, for it is in the present century that the importance of psychological as well as physical factors has come to be recognised. The requirement of modern industrial societies for raw materials, and especially rare metals and new sources of power, explains many of the highly complicated industrial groupings and activities of the present day. Above all is the basic requirement of food and the means of procuring this.

Given the purpose, the policy, and the motive force, the next step is to construct the administrative machine by which the required objective may be attained, and to drive it forward economically and efficiently. It is unfortunate, but inevitable, that the terminology used to describe these basically simple components of organisation and management has become complicated, for the process is essentially the same in any enterprise, be it large or small. Primitive man, confronted with an expanse of water and driven to cross it by fear or the urge for food, might seek for a ford, swim across it, or, if it was too vast, build himself a canoe or coracle. His modern counterpart would cross by a power-driven vessel or by aircraft, but the objective and motives would be the same, only the administrative process has become more complex. The fact remains, that *personnel* are still people, and *leadership* is still—leadership.

The chain of responsibility is recognisably similar in all large-scale organisations. At the top are those people who are, or should be, responsible for taking decisions, *i.e.* approving policy and ordering its execution. There may be one individual, or a group of men variously named, *e.g.* Cabinet, council, board of directors, and so on. At this level three things are required: firstly, a constant inflow of accurate information on which sound judgment can be based; secondly, the ability to see and define the problem as a whole and unobscured by administrative detail; and, thirdly, sufficient confidence and courage to give the necessary orders and leave others to carry them out.

It would be absurd to claim that this is all that is necessary. Any person, or group of persons, in command must also have a sense of awareness that only comes from great experience. If, for instance, an assessment of a given position does not "feel" right, it may be discovered that the statistical information on which it is based is faulty, not because of a failure in the most modern and expensive computing apparatus, but because the computor, the human being feeding information into the machine, was not feeling very well at the time, or was inexperienced in that particular piece of work. Henri Fayol,[1] a French industrialist, tried to analyse the qualities making for success, and he divided administration into various components such as organisation, command, co-ordination, and control. He is usually credited also with "planning", but, in fact, he used the word *prévoyance* from the French *prévoir*, to foresee. It is this quality of foresight that marks off the really great administrators. It is not, of course, implied that modern methods are inferior to the old "rule of thumb", but rather that anyone dealing with human affairs must pay due regard to many things not capable of scientific measurement. It is said that the manufacturers of a motor car of world-wide repute, when asked for information on the fine adjustment of a piece of mechanism, replied that they had no written standard, but that if one of their skilled mechanics said that it was properly adjusted, it was properly adjusted.

The quality of *prévoyance* is not a mysterious sixth sense with which some are endowed and others are not. It is true that some people are more sensitive and intelligent than others, but in general it is the ability to weigh up the situation in the light of past experience; hence the need for adequate and accurate factual information. The statistician and the economist have most important parts to play in an advisory capacity, provided it is realised that they can only speak in terms of trends. Occasionally they, like the meteorologists, can make a wrong forecast.

Having assessed the situation on the information available, and in the light of individual or collective experience, the next step is to formulate a policy or make a "plan". This, at the highest level, will consist of broad principles only, leaving the details to be filled in by others. A minister intent on introducing a national health service does not concern himself with the number of pills or tablets required per head of population, but rather with the broad outlines of administration, the relationships with medical, nursing, and ancillary services, and with the probable overall cost.

When policy has been determined it becomes necessary to ensure that an effective organisation exists to carry it out, subject always to sufficient central control being retained to ensure that any major departure from the original plan is referred back to the policy-making body for prior approval. The detailed execution of the

[1] Fayol, Henri, *Administration Industrielle et Générale*, 1916. English translation by Constance Storrs. *General and Industrial Management*, Pitman, 1949.

plan is the function of management, once defined as "getting things done through people".[1]

Here it is necessary to recall that scientific management is a product of the present century. Previously the managing clerk, or the manager of a business, gained his experience by growing up with the firm, or with one similar to it. There was no question of graduating from a school of business administration, or of acquiring a university degree, or a professional qualification, as a preliminary to taking up an administrative post. Personnel management, with its preoccupation with health and welfare, industrial psychology, accident prevention, vital and economic statistics, was almost unknown. So also were the problems of management services. The manager was the executive, public relations officer, and staff welfare officer all rolled into one. His place has been taken by a being of superior education, commonly known as a managing director, chief officer, or head of a department, who has under his control the various divisions of the organisation concerned.

The managing director is responsible to his board of directors, just as the chief officer of a local authority is responsible to his council, or the secretary of a hospital to the management committee. The outstanding quality required of the director, no matter what his official title may be, is leadership—a quality that is easily recognised when present, but difficult to define. A leader must have power, but possession of power does not create a leader. Many other things are necessary—initiative, integrity, imagination, mental stability, and, above all, the ability to inspire confidence and personal respect. It is impossible to respect a committee or board, or indeed to regard "them" as composed of human beings, although, oddly enough, it is sometimes possible to regard a government department as having certain individual characteristics, perhaps because of the anonymity of the civil servants composing it. Thus, one may have a high respect for one department and take a dim view of another, without knowing personally a single individual in them.

It is not necessary for a leader to inspire affection, but he must be prepared to accept responsibility at all times. A man or woman who is known always to be willing and able to do this earns the full confidence of the staff. A matron of one of the great teaching hospitals had the reputation of being a fearful dragon with her nurses, but her memory is respected to this day, for no one dared to criticise her staff, even by implication, without an immediate and personal assumption of responsibility on her part, even though she

[1] Urwick, L. F. *The Pattern of Management*, 1956, Pitman, p. 27.

had reduced the culprit to tears five minutes earlier. Loyalty to a leader, and confidence in him, are of the essence of good management.

It is at this level that human frailties become manifest in the administrative machine. The "herr direktor" who cannot delegate responsibility, but must supervise every process, the ineffective individual who is too small for the job, and the egotist who feels that he is too big, have their effect throughout the service. The former, the man who is not quite large enough for the job, cannot bring himself to trust others, for he does not wholly trust himself. His meticulous attention to detail may induce a state of anxiety in those around him, but, equally important, it may produce certain effects on himself, in the form of so-called "stress" diseases. The arrogant, over-bearing administrator, on the other hand, reduces those ill-starred enough to work under him to shadows, with equally unfortunate effects on their health and efficiency.

The quality of leadership, required of all men and women who accept executive responsibility, and who are placed in charge of others, is notoriously difficult to analyse. The ability to inspire confidence, the capacity for sustained effort, or "stickability", especially in adverse circumstances, honesty of purpose, and a willingness to shoulder the burden of decisions, all play their part in the making of a leader. But there are other, more ill-defined, factors, such as that little extra reserve of courage or energy to be drawn upon when others falter, that faculty of "awareness", *nous*, and common sense, which enables a dangerous situation to be visualised as a whole, and finally the combination of the man and the moment which can be called "luck".

The simplest form of organisation is, therefore, a pyramid of individuals, each with reasonably well-defined responsibilities, from the junior executive officer at the lowest level to the managing director at the top, who is, in turn, responsible to the body that determines and controls policy. At various levels in the chain of command may be found the specialists whose job it is to provide expert advice. These professional advisers may have subsidiary administrative responsibilities for their own section of work, but they do not take a major part in the general managerial activities. Also outside the main framework of administration are the personal assistants and private secretaries of the higher administrative officers, although their work may be of great importance. The success or failure of this system turns primarily on the individuals concerned, and the words delegation, co-operation, co-ordination, means of communication, and inter-personal relations are frequently in use to denote what is required at all levels. The essential requirement, of course, is clear direction from the top.

Another form of administrative organisation is the replacement of the individual controller at certain levels by a group of persons forming a committee. The intention may be the wholly admirable one of sharing responsibility and accepting the collective wisdom of the group, but it may, and sometimes does, result in the reverse, for committees may behave both irresponsibly and stupidly.

Committees may be advisory or executive. Advisory committees can perform most valuable services in considering and reporting on specific problems, and they are to be found at all levels of the national life. Executive committees are a prominent feature of local government work and of certain nationalised activities such as the health services, but it is perhaps significant that they play little part in industry. There are several reasons for this. A committee is bound by its terms of reference much more rigidly than the individual administrator may be. It must also act collectively, which means, in effect, in accordance with the views of the majority of the members present on that particular occasion. Those members may be swayed by oratory, political considerations, sentiment (committees can be much more sentimental than their individual members), or even by boredom, fatigue, or the lateness of the hour. The committee system also offers opportunities for delay, by postponing for further consideration, or by referring back, which are denied to the individual.

Committees can add very considerably to the amount of work required, for, in addition to agendas, minutes, and standing orders, each item for consideration requires a verbal or written report by the officer concerned. They may also, if subservient, add to the power of the chairman or the permanent officers, and thus produce the type of man so well described by Sir Winston Churchill as "The zealous official, who does not care what is done so long as he is at the centre of it",[1] for, as Professor S. H. Beer said in *Treasury Control* in 1957, "power we may take to be the ability of someone to get his decisions accepted by others".

Business or commercial administration is, in essence, a simple chain of direct responsibility from one person to another. It is in local government and in the great nationalised industries that the committee system finds its principal place. The advocates of the committee system will point with pride to the workmanlike attitude of a committee meeting in privacy, as compared with the formalities required in open and public meetings of the governing body, and to the close association between officers and members at such

[1] Winston S. Churchill, *Marlborough*, Vol. 1 (1933), p. 276.

meetings. They will emphasise the value of informal discussion, and the speed with which detailed administration is conducted. In effect, executive committees may become very powerful indeed, especially when they prepare detailed measures of policy for confirmation by the parent organisation.

In view of the legal position that no individual member of the council of a local authority can legally be given powers to act on its behalf, the special arrangement arises whereby the officers can, in an emergency, consult the chairman of the appropriate committee, who may then decide to authorise a course of action and seek the approval of his committee at their next meeting. In effect, the chairman may come to play a dominant role, for he must, of necessity, know more about the conduct of its business than the other members, and it is his responsibility to act as the spokesman of the committee in the full meetings of the controlling body. A weak chairman may thus mean over-powerful officers, and a dominant chairman may reduce both committees and officers to a minor position.

Committees may also be classified as statutory or permissive. The former are, as the name implies, mandatory under an Act of Parliament, for example, the Education, Maternity and Child Welfare, Housing, and Finance Committees of a local authority. Permissive committees are those which are formed for convenience of administration. It will be evident that such committees may have either executive or advisory functions, or they may perform both.

A further distinction is between standing and special, or *ad hoc*, committees. Standing committees are appointed for an indefinite period, or with re-appointment on an annual basis, and they may form the backbone of the local administrative structure by reason of their continuity of existence. Special committees are usually appointed to consider a particular problem, or some new development, such as a planning committee to consider proposals for a new building, but these *ad hoc* committees sometimes tend to acquire a kind of spontaneous regeneration, whereby their life may be prolonged almost indefinitely.

The titles given to committees, such as Establishment, Works, and Finance, usually indicate fairly clearly the nature of the duties performed. There is also the widespread practice of establishing a General Purposes Committee to deal with residual matters which are not the concern of some special committee. In practice, this General Purposes Committee tends to become the most important, especially if combined with finance, and there is then the danger that it may become a kind of secret executive council, in which all important business is discussed in the absence of the press and public. In such an event, the full council may become a rubber stamp machine for the approval of decisions taken by its own committee.

Another defect of the committee system stems from the human weakness of referring difficulties to someone else, in this case by the formation of a sub-committee. Not only is a multiplicity of committees and sub-committees bad for efficient administration because of the load of work placed on officials, but it is also harmful because the chairman, the members, and the officers attached to it, tend to develop a loyalty to "their" committee rather than to the organisation as a whole. Unhealthy rivalries may spring up between committees, especially if their terms of reference are ill-defined, and the spectacle of the respective chairmen wrangling in public can be an unedifying one.

Although everyone pays lip-service to such sayings as "The fewer the better" and "The ideal committee is that composed of one person", the system is too deeply rooted to be abolished. At its worst it is time-wasting, inefficient, and extravagant, for individuals meeting as a body are notoriously less careful of other money than their own or, alternatively, they may decide on a measure of economy, often in small matters, which would be regarded as mean and ungracious in private life. At its best the committee system provides for the wisdom of its members to be expressed corporately. As an advisory body it is admirable.

As an efficient executive mechanism the committee has many disadvantages. It tends to waste much time on the minutiae of administration, instead of making the decisions on broad planning and policy that one would expect of a board of directors. It lends itself to duplication of effort, which becomes increasingly lacking in co-ordination as the committees multiply in number. Finally, the committee system is inherently and structurally incapable of rapid action, initiative, and driving force. The drag of inertia is powerful, and the rate of acceleration is slow.

It is not without significance that the more recent developments in local government in the United States of America and elsewhere include the appointment of a City Manager as head of the administration, and responsible to an elected council which makes decisions on policy.

No system of organisation can be expected to work efficiently without competent organisers, whether they be called directors, managers, officials, or administrative officers. It is worth while, therefore, to consider for a few moments the qualifications required of such men. In the past it was sufficient for many to have been self-taught, and the "self-made man" was regarded, certainly by himself, as a model for others. It is now recognised that the competent administrator requires a sound basic education, preferably followed by a period at a university, in addition to specialised knowledge of his subject. The nature of that knowledge, and the methods of acquiring it, must vary with the work involved.

A manager in a commercial undertaking must be experienced, among other things, in general administration methods of accountancy, store-keeping, advertising, the law relating to companies and contracts, and the like, as well as in the special manufacturing processes under his general management. The government servant is no longer content with a knowledge of the methods of working of his own department. Many have a wider general knowledge of certain subjects than the experts with whom they deal. Within a ministry of health, for example, there is usually an unrivalled body of knowledge on the administration of health services, and similar expertise may be found in many other central departments.

CHAPTER VI

VOLUNTARY ORGANISATIONS AND PUBLIC
CORPORATIONS

It might well be asked why a chapter on voluntary organisations is included in a book on the Art of Administration. There are several reasons, of which perhaps the most important is that every reform must begin as a voluntary effort on the part of someone. If a small group of persons feels sufficiently strongly about a matter they will meet and organise themselves into a body. After a period of time, if they persist, sufficient financial backing may become available to enable professional workers and administrators to be engaged. A "local" movement may become national, and attract the interest of ministers and of Parliament. National policy may be thereby affected, or the Government may adopt the service and make it statutory upon the local authorities to provide it. Alternatively, the particular service may come to be regarded as so important that it is authorised by Parliament on a national or regional basis, and thus weaken the traditional "all-purpose" local authority pattern. Another reason for considering voluntary effort in this context is that without it a modern state could only be administered as a bureaucracy, with paid officials replacing the voluntary organisations and the committee system.

It may be said, without undue exaggeration, that every aspect of national life has had its origins in voluntary effort. The local government framework, and the local administration of the law, could not have been evolved without the aid over many centuries of the voluntary justices of the peace. The educational system has its roots in the foundation of the ancient universities and colleges, the charitable foundations which later became public schools, and the early grammar schools. The founders of the public dispensaries and hospitals for the care of the sick in the eighteenth century may, or may not, have been aware that they were re-building on the pattern of medical care of the monastic infirmaries, but they certainly never foresaw the day when a minister of health might take over the administration of hospitals as part of a national health service. Indeed, the whole system of present-day administration derives from structures evolved by voluntary movements. The intrusion of central government activities into the personal affairs of the people during the present century has been taken by many people to mark the end of voluntary effort. Experience has already shown that this is not the case, and it is worth while examining for a moment the motives which led to these activities.

It becomes apparent, when reading the works of the early reformers that they, and those who came to support them, were actuated by three main motives, fear, altruism, and economic necessity, and these may be applied more generally. Fear is a powerful spur, whether it be fear of loss of personal liberties, of some great killing disease such as cholera, or of some new and unknown hazard such as the effects of radio-active materials. Altruism, or compassion for others, forms the basis of all the great religions, and it is a fundamental part of the ethics of the Christian faith. Its power to be effective depends very much on the state of knowledge of a community. For many centuries compassion for the sick and suffering was limited to charitable care, as the morbid processes underlying disease were not understood. Economic necessity may be the stimulus by which voluntary effort receives practical support. Before the early hospitals could be founded, it was necessary to demonstrate that they would be useful to the community, and that enquiry into the causes of disease and affording better treatment might lead to the prolongation of life. This prolongation of life became more important in industrial communities, whose survival depended on the output of skilled craftsmen. It was a hard-headed philanthropy that led to the support of some early voluntary efforts.

Perhaps the best modern example of the influence of these three factors of fear, altruism, and economic necessity, may be seen in the foundation of the great international organisations since the end of the Second World War. The fear of the spread of disease, compassion for the sick and hungry, especially in the backward areas of the world, and economic demands, have all played their part.

In effect, it is the role of voluntary effort to pioneer new ventures, and to fill the gaps in the public services until such time as the State may be prepared to act. Voluntary organisations paved the way for State intervention in the relief of the poor, the sick, mothers and young children, the aged, the handicapped, in education and housing, the care of delinquents and social outcasts, to name only a few of the activities on which public money amounting to many millions of pounds is now spent each year.

Many voluntary organisations remain entirely dependent on private subscriptions and donations, and take pride in the fact that they are not assisted by the State in any way. Some are supported in part by local public funds, while others become sufficiently valuable to the nation to attract grants from the central government. The wheel has even gone so far in its revolution that voluntary bodies have been created, or promoted, by central government departments to explore and pave the way for possible future developments.

In addition to their value as pioneers, and in filling in the gaps in existing services, or in moulding and influencing government policy, voluntary organisations are important because of the types of workers they employ and their training. Many of the "official" workers can trace their origins, and their technical education, to the voluntary efforts of the last century. The organisations responsible for the coming into being of trained social workers, health visitors, district nurses and midwives, all arose from voluntary societies, as did also the specialised agencies for the physically and mentally handicapped.

Voluntary societies and charitable institutions may be numbered in thousands. Some are of ancient foundation and purely local in character, such as the various charities for providing money and food for the needy or for the provision of alms-houses. Even here, curiously enough, the State is concerned, for the long experience of the care of the elderly in alms-houses has tended to influence the siting and design of flats and dwellings for the aged, provided by local authorities and approved by the central government.

Other organisations may operate on a wider, even national basis, and with religious inspiration. This is particularly the case with the various moral welfare societies, concerned with the care and protection of girls and young women, and with the unmarried mother. So valuable is this work that nearly all local authorities aid these societies with substantial grants, as the best way of dealing with this difficult form of personal service.

Some voluntary bodies, national in character, are concerned with a particular purpose, such as the care of the blind, the care of cripples, marriage guidance, and mental health. It is societies such as these that exert a powerful influence in shaping public opinion, and thereby lead to action by governments. Some act as agents for the central or local government authorities, for example, in maintaining holiday homes and residential schools for invalid and handicapped children.

An example of societies engaged in general social work is the National Council of Social Service, which acts as a co-ordinating body, and also as a link between the central government and voluntary activities in Britain. It provides the national headquarters for the citizen's advice bureaux, rural community councils concerned with the welfare of people in rural areas, local councils of social service which study the social problems of their area and mobilise local resources to deal with them, old people's welfare committees, and the like. This national council also provides the secretariat for many other voluntary groups, and serves as the agency for associating these various activities with international work, government departments, local authorities, and, most important, with each other. Without such co-ordination there is a serious risk of overlapping and duplication of effort.

A nice example of evolution in the social field is the Family Welfare Association, founded in England in 1869 as the Charity Organisation Society. At that time poverty was severe and wide-spread, and the Charity Organisation Society was concerned with what was called rescue work, that is, the setting of the individual on his feet again. Now that this kind of charitable relief is no longer necessary, the Association concentrates on the family problems, such as chronic invalidism, housing, and matrimonial difficulties. There is now a number of agencies engaged on family case work of various kinds.

Among the wartime agencies which have continued to function in peacetime is the Women's Royal Voluntary Services, subsidised by the central government, and engaged in relief work in emergencies, or as part of civil defence, and in the welfare of the aged and sick (including, for example, the "Meals on Wheels" service). There are also the citizen's advice bureaux, mentioned above, which were founded to meet the problems of citizens rendered homeless by bombing.

Finally, there are the international voluntary agencies, such as the Red Cross, which operate also on a national and local basis. Founded as a result of Henri Dunant's experiences on the battlefield of Solferino, in 1859, the Red Cross retains its major interest in the care of the sick and wounded in times of war and disaster, but it is also active in the health and welfare field, and is particularly interested in the care of crippled children, the disabled, and the aged.

There has been much speculation in recent years about the future of voluntary societies now that so many material needs have been met by the State. But although the State can provide the framework, and the material and financial resources, it is the spirit of voluntary effort that makes welfare work succeed locally. Personal interest in the sick and infirm, and in hospitals, by voluntary bodies, enable amenities to be provided, improvements to be made, and lonely patients to be befriended. This is particularly important in mental hospitals and in institutions for the mentally sub-normal.

Some organisations operate canteens for out-patients and their relatives, trolley-shops and libraries for in-patients, and assume responsibility for the care of linen.

A most important field of voluntary effort is in the various youth services, and some of the organisations engaged in this work have now quite a long history. The Young Men's Christian Association was founded in 1844, and the Young Women's Christian Association in 1855. Similarly, the Girls' Friendly Society, the Boys' Brigade, and the Church Lads' Brigade, all date from the last century, while the Boy Scouts and Girl Guides Associations were founded early in the present century. More recent developments have been the national associations of youth clubs, designed to provide recreational facilities for young men and women, with particular reference to their mental, physical, and spiritual well-being. Voluntary agencies with similar aims are the Outward Bound Trust, with its mountain and sea schools and courses designed to encourage self-reliance and self-discipline, the Youth Hostels Association, the Central Council for Physical Recreation, which is grant-aided by the Ministry of Education and Science, and the National Playing Fields Association. More specialised are organisations such as the National Federation of Young Farmers' Clubs.

The importance of youth services in education was recognised early in this century by what was then the Board of Education (now the Ministry of Education and Science), and it has received statutory recognition in the Education Acts. Local education authorities are now required to ensure that adequate facilities exist in their areas for the recreational and social needs of young people, and they are empowered to give financial assistance to voluntary youth organisations for this purpose.

It is not an exaggeration to say that voluntary societies exist in connection with all aspects of corporate or community life, and their activities become interwoven with the fabric of administration. Such is the case, for example, with the after-care of prisoners, who are assisted on discharge from prison by local and voluntary bodies supported partly by private and partly by public funds. The work of the local societies is co-ordinated by a national association. Prisoners discharged from certain prisons in Britain are generally subject to statutory supervision, and are cared for by a voluntary body financed from public funds, with a council appointed by the Home Secretary. This organisation works through local associates, usually probation officers (in Scotland through voluntary guardians), who "advise, assist, and befriend" the discharged prisoner for as long as is required.

Social Workers

It is necessary to turn now to the consideration of the social workers employed by these various agencies. When first established, voluntary societies were mainly concerned with what would to-day be called case work, *i.e.* concentration upon the individual. This is still often so with many societies, such as those concerned with the care of spastic children, or with the welfare of old people. Then came the emphasis on providing for group activities for special purposes—social, educational, or recreational. Finally, there developed the community organisation, concerned with the mobilisation and co-ordination of local resources to meet the needs of a community. Many of these developments have led to the employment of specialised social workers, some of whom now undergo technical or university training, which is recognised by a diploma or a degree.

In other instances a university degree in the arts or in social science is recognised as a desirable qualification, to be followed by some specialised training within the particular service. Yet again, many workers are recruited on their general academic and personal qualities, and depend entirely on "in-service" training and experience for their subsequent skill.

One general trend is quite clear. The voluntary part-time helper is increasingly giving way to the full-time salaried worker trained in the principles and techniques of his subject. By reason of historical accident there has developed in some countries an extraordinary multiplicity of these workers, each with his own title and special interest, in sharp contrast to the basic simplicity of, for instance, the French polyvalent "Assistantes Sociales".

When voluntary activities were purely local, little difficulty arose, but with the growth of national activities there is an urgent need to study the training and functions of social workers. This is the more important now that government departments and local authorities employ so many social workers of various kinds. They include, for example, welfare officers, children's officers, youth leaders, housing managers, probation officers, and workers in the health services.

Government servants may be required in the course of their work to act in a disciplinary or controlling capacity. Thus, a professionally-trained social worker employed in the government service may have to act as an inspector, whose report may lead to withdrawing or withholding of a grant, discontinuing some local activity, or supporting a local authority in the dismissal of an official. While, therefore, they can, and do, make valuable and constructive suggestions, based on a wide experience, to improve the efficiency of the organisations with which they deal, there is always the knowledge that their primary loyalty is to the central authority which may, in the last resort, have to apply statutory powers or enforce a statutory duty.

Truly voluntary organisations, unaided by public money, are free from restrictions of this kind. In others, the relatively small amount of financial aid they receive may not imply anything more than an interest by the central or local government department in keeping the voluntary activity healthy, as being of benefit to the community. Where, however, the government has come to play a major part in the work of a voluntary organisation by making substantial grants to it, then, sooner or later, the stage is reached when the organisation ceases to be "voluntary" and becomes "public". Many national advisory bodies are of this nature. They are voluntary in that the members of the governing board or committee are unpaid, but some or all of them may be appointed by the minister, civil servants may "sit in" on meetings, or attend as observers or assessors, and the organisation and finance may, if occasion arises, be the subject of official enquiry. The voluntary organisation has become a public body, and it is only a step from this to the public corporation.

Public Corporations

A phenomenon of the present century has been the development of the public corporations, which are public bodies established to operate major industries and services in the public interest, such as coal mining, gas supply, electricity generation and supply, civil air transport, and the railways.

Some of these public corporations are so large and powerful that their relations with ministers are as yet ill-defined. The chairman of a vast nationalised industry, for example, may expect to be able to deal direct with the responsible minister and not with what he might regard as minor officials. The minister, on the other hand, may be in the difficult position of having to defend the corporation and its policy, the government and its policy, his own department, and, no less important, himself. The principal means of control lies in the power of appointment by the minister of auditors to the boards and councils, the right to make regulations and to give specific directions, and the power to hold public enquiries and to settle disputes. There is also the power to seek for detailed information, either by enquiry or through an inspectorate. Ministers are also given a general mandate to secure effective co-ordination. Financial control is exercised, both as regards disposal of profits, and in the provision of loans.

Voluntary effort may be seen in these public corporations also, by way of advisory committees and consumers' councils.

Where the minister assumes direct responsibility to Parliament for a new social service rather different considerations arise. On 5 July 1948, the Minister of Health became the head of an organisation which aimed "to promote the establishment in England and Wales of a comprehensive health service designed to secure improvement in the physical and mental health of the people of England and Wales and the prevention, diagnosis, and treatment of illness, and for that purpose to provide or secure the effective provision of services". In order to do so he took over, on behalf of Parliament, the hospitals. These had hitherto been administered by a variety of voluntary bodies and local authorities, and they comprised institutions of many kinds, including general hospitals, mental hospitals, maternity homes, infectious diseases hospitals, sanatoria, mental deficiency institutions, and convalescent homes. To administer them, Regional Hospital Boards were created, with separate Boards of Governors for the teaching hospitals. Members of these Boards are appointed by the minister, and they, in turn, appoint the members of the hospital management committees, which carry on the day-to-day administration of the hospitals. The members are unpaid, and they differ from local authority members in being selected and not elected. The Boards also differ from local authorities in other respects. They have no major source of income except from central funds, and the hospitals, land, property, and equipment, all belong to the minister. It is, therefore, truly a national service, but the Boards are separate legal entities with their own statutory duties and responsibilities. Central financial control is strict, and salaries and conditions of service of staffs in hospitals are subject to central negotiation.

At its best, this type of organisation represents an ideal form of partnership between the State and voluntary effort, for only those with a sense of vocation can normally be expected to devote the vast amount of time which the unpaid membership of these boards and committees entails. Too rigid a control from the centre would remove all interest, and there would then be a danger that only the older members of the community would have the necessary time or patience to carry out the minister's instructions. Fortunately, that state of affairs has not arisen. If it did, an alternative would be to transfer responsibility for the National Health Service to a public corporation.

CHAPTER VII

UNIVERSITY ADMINISTRATION

The administration of universities is worthy of study for several reasons. In the first place, the history of university education is, in effect, that of the evolution of educational services generally; secondly, the universities, by reason of their place at the apex of the pyramid of education, provide many of the teachers and administrators of the country; and, thirdly, the method whereby universities in Britain have maintained their independence in spite of ever increasing financial aid from public funds is an excellent example of what can be done with goodwill on both sides.

The early history of universities in Britain, as in other parts of Europe, dates back to the revival of learning in the twelfth and thirteenth centuries, and the word is derived from *universitas*, meaning a guild or corporation. When foreign-born scholars were expelled from the University of Paris, in 1167, some of them settled in Oxford and helped to found a university. When a further migration of teachers and scholars occurred from Oxford, in 1209, they settled in Cambridge, attracted, in part no doubt, by the ecclesiastical foundations already in existence there, as well as by the peaceful and pleasant situation.

The characteristic development of Oxford and Cambridge Universities began early, when pious benefactors founded residential halls for teachers and students, a process which started in the thirteenth century and still continues. This collegiate system, whereby the university has its own identity and constitution, but in which the colleges are corporate bodies governed by their own Fellows, and are autonomous so far as property, finances, and internal affairs are concerned, is at first sight confusing.

In effect, it is the university which confers degrees, and sets the standards required to attain these. It owns the central libraries and laboratories, and employs the teachers engaged in formal teaching —professors, readers, university lecturers, and demonstrators. The colleges provide the vital centres of academic life within the university. The student can enter the university only by being accepted as a member of a college. For a considerable part of his student life he lives in the college, and he dines regularly throughout each term in the communal college hall where the head of the college and the senior members sit at the high table.

The communal life of the college centres, as in monastic times, round the chapel (although attendance is no longer obligatory), the college library, the hall, and the college living and common rooms. Much informal teaching and advice is given by the senior members of the college, and especially by the tutors and directors of studies, many of whom are themselves young men. The corporate life of the college, and the tutorial system of informal instruction in small groups, play an important part in moulding the personal and intellectual character of the undergraduates, and for many centuries the men so trained became the leaders of Church and State, the Law and Medicine. When the Civil Service Commission was set up, in 1855, the commissioners based the syllabus of the examinations for the administrative class (*q.v.*) on the curricula of the universities, particularly of Oxford and Cambridge, and these universities still supply a high proportion of the entrants to this class of the Civil Service, although the numbers recruited from other universities have increased considerably since the Second World War.

In medieval times, the teaching of the liberal arts included the *trivium*—grammar, logic, and rhetoric—and the *quadrivium*—arithmetic, geometry, music, and astronomy. To these were added the higher faculties of theology, law, and medicine. Written examinations for degrees were not introduced until 1772, and both universities shared in the reforms characteristic of the early nineteenth century.

The next development of university education in Britain was the founding of the three Scottish universities, St Andrews, Glasgow, and Aberdeen in the fifteenth century, and a fourth, Edinburgh, in the sixteenth century. The collegiate system was not adopted by these universities, and the emphasis there has always been placed on the intellectual, rather than the social, aspects of university life. With this has been associated the fiercely maintained independence of the students to live their own lives.

The third phase of university development is illustrated by the founding of the universities of London, Durham, and Wales, which have federal constitutions. London, now the largest university in Britain, was constituted by Royal Charter in 1836 as a body empowered to examine and confer degrees on students of approved institutions. In 1858 its degrees were made available to external students, both at home and overseas, and in 1878 it became the first university in the United Kingdom to admit women to its degrees.

The fourth stage of development in university education in Britain is that of the "civic" universities of the present century. Beginning in the eighteenth and nineteenth centuries as literary and philosophical societies, often with university extension courses and lectures from Oxford and Cambridge, there developed university colleges designed to provide higher education for the people of the area in which they were situated. By their nature they were non-residential, and they usually owed their inception to local bene-factions.

At first these colleges had strong local interests, with particular emphasis on science and technology, and students were prepared for the external degrees of London University. University status followed later, often with the local schools of medicine forming the nucleus of the faculty of medicine. Since the Second World War, this process has been accelerated. By reason of their history, these universities are essentially non-collegiate and non-residential, although students are drawn from all parts of the country and, indeed, from all parts of the world.

It is noteworthy that in the recognition of women the process of evolution has been reversed. Women have been given full status in all civic universities since their foundation. In the case of the University of London they were given full status in 1878, in the universities of Scotland in 1892, Durham in 1896, Oxford in 1920, and in Cambridge in 1948.

The ancient universities derived the authority for their founda-tion from Papal Bulls. To-day, all universities obtain their rights and powers from Royal Charters which define the powers, privi-leges, and constitution of the university in outline. Supplementary to the charter, and reinforcing it, are the university statutes. Subsidiary to the Royal Charter and the statutes are the ordin-ances, decrees, graces, and regulations governing the day-to-day administration.

Although the administration of the universities varies in detail, a common pattern may be seen in them all. At the head is a chancellor, a person distinguished in academic or public life, who is elected by the university and who usually holds office for life. The chancellor may preside at formal meetings of the governing body of the university and at the congregations where degrees are conferred, or he may delegate these responsibilities to the vice-chancellor, except on special occasions, as when honorary degrees are conferred. The vice-chancellor is the chief academic and administrative officer, and he may hold office permanently or for a period of two to four years.

The chief executive officer is usually entitled the registrar, or registrary, and it is his responsibility to keep the official records and lists of members, and to see that the statutes and ordinances are obeyed. At Oxford and Cambridge special officers, known as proctors, are appointed to maintain discipline. Their assistants are familiarly known as "bulldogs".

In addition to the registrar, the other chief officials may include one whose main purpose is to co-ordinate the academic business of the university, with some such title as secretary-general of the faculties, and also a chief finance officer or treasurer.

For academic purposes related studies are grouped in faculties, and the work of these is co-ordinated by a central body, commonly the senate or the general board of the faculties. Financial affairs are delegated by the charter or statutes to another central body, usually the council or the financial board. The highest governing body has various titles in different universities, but is most often known as the court.

It is in the detailed pattern of administration that the main differences between universities are to be found, and many of these have arisen because of the variations in history. Whereas the ancient universities developed from a medieval guild or corporation of teachers and students, with a monastic pattern of communal life, the modern universities represent equally well the needs of the type of society in which they have been founded. In the former, the government of the university may be entirely domestic. Administration, finance, and academic policy are, in fact, controlled by the resident senior members of the university. In the Scottish universities the final authority rests in the hands of the court, a small body which includes the rector of the university, the principal, and the Lord Provost of the city.

In the federal universities, the constituent colleges and institutions have freedom to manage their own affairs, with central control of university policy and finance. In London, the court includes representatives of the senate, persons nominated by the Crown, and nominees of the local authorities, and it controls finance. The senate deals with academic matters, including appointments to the teaching staffs. In Wales the pattern is similar, but the court is very large, members being drawn from the local authorities and public bodies in Wales, in addition to graduate members of the university.

The civic universities, while preserving this general pattern, reflect in their administration the local interests which supported them in their formation. The supreme governing body, the court, represents a wide range of interests, e.g. other universities, local authorities, educational organisations, learned societies, and religious denominations. The court appoints the majority of the members of the council, which controls all the business of the university and it also appoints the vice-chancellor. The strong representation of business men on the councils, and others with wide practical experience of administration, has been of great material benefit to those universities. The senate is the academic body, mainly composed of the professors, which co-ordinates the work of the faculties. It is subject to the powers of the council, but, in practice, the latter very rarely interferes with academic policy.

It is this complex pattern of university administration that has to be borne in mind when considering the financial relationships with the central government, for of the total annual income of British universities over 80 per cent. is derived directly from central funds.

This central financial aid is the product of the present century, for it was not until 1919 that a standing committee was appointed by the Chancellor of the Exchequer to enquire into the financial needs of university education in the United Kingdom, and to advise the government as to the application of any grants to be made by Parliament towards meeting them. That committee is known as the University Grants Committee.

After the Second World War the terms of reference of the University Grants Committee were revised, and are now concerned with the co-ordinated development of the universities as well as with the distribution of grants. The committee has a staff of civil servants with its own administrative structure, under the general supervision of the Treasury. The chairman and secretary are full-time officers, and the other members of the committee are part-time and serve for a limited term of years.

The success of this method of financial administration, whereby funds voted by Parliament are administered by an independent committee and the freedom of the universities is preserved, turns on two main factors. Firstly, there is the general recognition that the quality of university work, and the calibre of new graduates entering the public service and industry, would suffer if freedom to experiment and develop in new directions were hampered. Secondly, the method of working of the University Grants Committee is favourable to continuity of effort. The universities prepare their estimates on a five-yearly basis. Shortly before each quinquennium members of the University Grants Committee visit and discuss in detail with the central bodies, the heads of university departments, and other teaching officers, their programmes for the future. These visits have the double merit of ensuring that plans for expansion are carefully prepared, and equally carefully scrutinised. The individual programmes are then combined, by the university authorities, into a detailed estimate of income and expenditure for the university as a whole during the next quinquennium. These estimates from all universities are consolidated by the University Grants Committee into its recommendations to the Treasury. The Chancellor of the Exchequer advises Parliament of the amount needed, and an appropriate sum is then voted. The University Grants Committee allocates money from this to the universities as a grant for each of the ensuing five years.

It should be noted that the universities receive a block grant which they may spend as they wish, but some items of expenditure, such as academic salaries, must fall within certain limits, for they are to a large extent nationally determined. Naturally, no university would embark on heavy new expenditure for which it had not prepared in advance estimates of which the University Grants Committee were aware, but five years is a reasonable time for which to plan ahead.

Somewhat similar procedure governs non-recurrent grants for capital expenditure, for instance, on sites, buildings, and equipment. These are assessed on an annual basis, but well in advance. Universities are, of course, free to supplement their income from other sources, including public contributions, the great philanthropic foundations, or their own monies. Because of the heavy investment of public money in university education, Parliament has now decided that university accounts must be open to scrutiny by the Comptroller and Auditor-General.

Nearly all full-time students in British universities are now being assisted from public funds, either as state scholars or by way of local authority grants and scholarships. It is relevant, when considering the art of administration, to note that where the Government service, the public corporations, commerce, and industry, all compete financially to attract the best young men and women emerging from the universities, there is a danger that only the second best may be left to teach either in schools or in the universities themselves.

CHAPTER VIII

THE MACHINERY OF GOVERNMENT

When a country is engaged primarily in agriculture, the population is scattered, and large towns are few in number. The needs of the people are relatively simple, and the central government carries out its administrative functions on a territorial basis, by sub-divisions such as provinces or counties, which may in turn be sub divided into units as small as an individual parish. The towns, important because they are the seat of government or because they have a market, a port, a fortress, or a university, may have their own organisation. The successful administration of such a country depends upon the strength or weakness of the central government.

In England, in medieval times, the country was divided into counties, each of which had a principal officer, the sheriff, appointed by the Crown. The sheriff was so powerful that the great writer on constitutional history, Maitland, spoke of him as being, in effect, "a provincial viceroy". Strong central control was also exercised by peripatetic judges known as the justices in eyre. These men visited each county armed with a long list of questions known as the articles of the eyre, and conducted a detailed inquisition into the delinquencies and short-comings both of the community and of individuals within it.

The sheriffs and the justices in eyre became very unpopular. When the office of coroner was created, in 1194, some of the duties of enquiries, particularly into the cause of violent or unnatural death, devolved upon him, but it was the appointment of conservators of the peace by Edward III which laid the foundation of an effective local administration. In 1359, justices of the peace were given powers to enforce the Statute of Labourers, and in 1361 the Justices of the Peace Act gave them statutory powers in addition to those already held by virtue of their commission from the Crown. With the passage of time these justices became the principal local administrative officers. As they were appointed by the Crown, their activities were controlled to a very considerable extent by the Privy Council. The justices would act either individually, as two or more in a court of petty sessions, or the justices of the whole county sitting in quarter sessions. Thus, one justice might order relief for a pauper, two or more in petty sessions might licence an ale-house, while all the justices in quarter sessions might be called

71

upon to raise the county rates to enable a bridge or a gaol to be built.

It will be evident that local government was vested in the hands of men appointed by the Crown, men who were liable to summary dismissal if they failed to obey instructions from the King in Council, with the Court of Star Chamber as the judicial enforcing body. Had this court not been abolished, in 1640, during the struggle with the Stuart kings, it is possible that local government as it is now understood in Britain would never have evolved.

Fortunately, the long struggle for the supremacy of Parliament, beginning with Magna Carta in 1215, and proceeding by way of the Petition of Right in 1628, the Bill of Rights of 1689, and the Act of Settlement, 1701, was successful. Government by the royal prerogative became government by and through Parliament, with a constitutional monarchy.

For a time the pendulum now swung in the reverse direction, and during the eighteenth century the justices of the peace conducted "the county business" unhampered by central control, with the clerk of the peace as their chief officer. The results were sometimes unfortunate, particularly for the poor, as, for example, when the county justices of Berkshire fixed, in 1795, a harsh scale for the relief of paupers, a decision sometimes known as the "Speenhamland Act of Parliament".

Although the central government did not exercise its powers of control, the judges of the High Court of Justice could, and did, and especially the Court of King's Bench, by way of the ancient prerogative writs of *mandamus, prohibition,* and *certiorari.* By these means, the judges could prevent the local justices from exceeding their powers, or compel them to take action. The control was, however, incomplete, for only the wealthy could invoke the aid of the Court of King's Bench, and the latter was bound by its own previous decisions. The control was a legal one, and allowed little room for flexibility.

During the eighteenth century, also, the industrial revolution had resulted in extraordinary changes in the distribution of the population. Small country towns in the midlands and north of England became large cities, with no effective machinery of administration. To the inefficient county justices, therefore, were added special improvement commissioners for these cities, created by local Acts of Parliament for various special purposes, such as the paving and draining of streets, lighting, and the maintenance of order. Other *ad hoc* bodies were established in the eighteenth century to deal with the relief of the poor, usually by way of workhouses, and to maintain the turnpikes or highways.

Not only was the pattern of local administration confused, but the principle had become established that the central government would under no circumstances interfere with local government, however inefficient this might be, especially in the new industrial towns. The time was ripe for reform, and the Poor Law Act, 1834, reimposed central control by the appointment of the Poor Law Commissioners, who were officials of the central government. In the following year, 1835, the Municipal Corporations Act reformed the administration of the boroughs, with elected councils. Power thus passed from the property owners to the ratepayers, and from the local justices to elected councillors and their officers.

The attempts at reform, and the need to maintain stringent central powers of inspection and control, led to a multiplicity of authorities for health, education, highways, the poor law, and like matters, and it was not until the problems of reform became so urgent as to brook no further delay that attempts at simplification became successful. Under the great Public Health Act of 1875, for example, the country was divided into urban and rural sanitary districts, while the Local Government Act of 1888 transferred to newly-created county councils the administrative functions hitherto performed by the justices of the peace sitting in quarter sessions. This Act also created county boroughs by relieving certain large cities of responsibility to the county, and giving to the town councils all the powers of a county within their own boundaries.

The Local Government Act of 1894 brought the sanitary authorities into this new framework by the creation of urban and rural district councils. This Act also made provision for parish meetings and parish councils in rural districts. In 1902, education was brought into line by the Education Act of that year, and from then onwards all forms of local government were carried on by statutory local authorities. Even the guardians of the poor were abolished, by the Local Government Act of 1929, and their duties transferred to county and county borough councils. The next step, after creating uniformity of local authorities, was to simplify the laws from which they derived their powers, and from 1934 to the outbreak of the Second World War in 1939 a number of codifying statutes were passed, designed to consolidate and simplify the laws under which local government services were operated.

Meanwhile, the process of central control had taken a new and rather menacing turn, and here it is necessary to return for a moment to the rise of Parliamentary supremacy. *Danby's Case*, in 1679 (11 St. Tr. 599), had helped to establish the principle that a minister of state cannot shelter himself from legal responsibility by a plea of obedience to the command of the Sovereign, and from the time of the Bill of Rights in 1689 ministers became increasingly responsible to Parliament for their actions. They were also held to be liable in law for their acts. While, therefore, the monarch can do no wrong, a minister and those acting under him who commit a wrong in the course of executing the Queen's business are personally liable in law, and can make the Crown responsible in law for their illegal acts and omissions.

In addition to this legal responsibility, each minister is responsible to Parliament for every act, error, or omission of his department. Only the minister can answer in Parliament, and it is his duty to shield the civil servants who advise him. In theory, therefore, the position is that, as Parliament makes the laws, and as ministers are directly answerable to Parliament for their acts, no minister can exceed the powers given to him by Parliament.

With the vast extension of government responsibility, especially during the present century, Parliament has no longer either the time or the knowledge required for detailed administration. All it can hope to do is to lay down certain broad general principles and leave the ministers to implement these. The National Health Service Act of 1946, for example, enabled a national health service to be brought into being, but the Minister of Health controls it by way of statutory rules and orders and the less formal correspondence of the civil servants within his Ministry.

This legislative power delegated by Parliament to ministers may have various names, for example, Orders in Council, regulations, rules, orders, schemes, or by-laws, and their general effect has been to increase enormously the power of the central government departments at the expense of local government. The central position may be strengthened still further by the system of financial aid by way of block grants and the like. The pendulum is therefore swinging once more in favour of powerful central control at the expense of the autonomy of the local authorities. The position of the latter has been further weakened in recent years by the process of regional organisation, so valuable during the Second World War for emergency purposes, and by the development of the nationalised industries. Coal, gas, electricity, and hospitals, to name only a few, are administered on a regional basis, and so, in a little more than eighty years, the urban and rural district councils have seen their powers whittled away in favour of the larger counties and county boroughs, and these in turn have seen the loss of some of their functions to regional and national bodies. With the cost and complexity of modern services the process was inevitable, for the load, and the benefits, must be spread over wider areas, but there are disadvantages.

One result of this multiplicity of authorities has been an extraordinary extension of the committee system. Every controlling body—national, regional, or local—has its standing committees, some of which are statutory. In addition to these there are many committees set up *ad hoc* to deal with special matters. Committee procedure has, therefore, become of great importance, for the whole fabric of administration may depend upon it, and there are very few people now who could claim to be entirely untrammelled by administrative measures.

It will be evident that, in order to make a complex administrative machine work smoothly, more is required than a framework rigid enough to support its load yet sufficiently flexible to permit of progress. In addition, the people must be sufficiently well disciplined to accept needed restrictions, and intelligent enough to play their part.

Reference has already been made to the checks and balances evolved over the centuries between the executive, the legislature, and the Courts of Law. The rise of modern local government was touched upon and also the trend towards regional organisations. In this chapter the component parts of the administrative machine will be discussed in more detail.

The relationships between these three components vary from country to country. In Britain, for example, the Queen is a constitutional monarch, and must, therefore, act on the advice of her ministers. She has, however, the ultimate responsibility of accepting, and if need be of forcing, the resignation of the government of the day and inviting other ministers to replace it. Needless to say, that power is exercised only in the normal constitutional manner, but it is an assurance of residual strength which is an extremely valuable safeguard.

In the Middle Ages the monarch was the owner of all land. He could not be sued in his own courts, and as there was no one superior to him he could not be sued at all. He was also head of the State, and recognised as having certain powers, additional to those of the other lords, which were necessary to preserve the State against enemies, and which should be used only for the public benefit. These powers were known as the royal prerogative.

The long contest in the seventeenth century, in which Charles I lost his life and James II was expelled from the country, ended in the recognition that the monarch had certain essential powers, for example, to summon and dissolve Parliament, or to declare war and make peace, but as parliamentary government had become more stable and responsible these prerogative powers could be exercised only through ministers who were themselves answerable to Parliament.

To-day the prerogative powers are those recognised by law as belonging to the Crown. They are not laid down by any statute, but are survivals from the past which have been retained.

It should be noted here that the term "the Crown" means both Queen and government, so that the prerogative powers are now exercised also by the ministers composing the government. Ministers of the Crown are appointed by the Queen on the nomination of the Prime Minister. A minister is usually recognised as being one of the great political Officers of State, with a department responsible to him, but there are also junior ministers holding subordinate positions.

Many of the prerogative powers have been replaced by statutes, but quite a number remain. Thus, by virtue of the prerogative, the Queen summons, prorogues, and dissolves Parliament, on the advice of her ministers. All criminal prosecutions are brought in the name of the Crown, and the Crown may stop a prosecution by the exercise of prerogative power by the Attorney-General. The Crown may also pardon convicted offenders on the advice of the Home Secretary. The Royal Navy is a prerogative force, maintained without statutory authority, whereas the Army and the Royal Air Force depend for their existence on an Act of Parliament that has to be renewed each year.

Appointments to all posts in the Civil Service are to the service of the Crown, and the Queen is also responsible for the appointment of judges of the Supreme Court, the principal officers of the Church, and the conferring of honours and decorations. All these are prerogative powers, and there are also important prerogatives to be used in times of national emergency.

It will be seen, therefore, that these wide powers, although much reduced from former times, are still of great importance. They help to account also for the power of the ministers.

As noted above, ministers are appointed by the Crown on the recommendation of the Prime Minister. They are, almost invariably, members of the political party in office, and it has long been one of the conventions of the British Constitution that Cabinet Ministers, that is to say, the principal ministers of the Crown who are invited to sit in the Cabinet by the Prime Minister, assume collective responsibility for all acts of the government. It would be unthinkable for a Cabinet Minister to remain in office and vote against the government, or even to say that he is in disagreement with it. On the contrary, he must defend government policy whenever necessary. In addition, each minister is individually responsible to the Queen and to Parliament for the conduct of his department.

Major questions of policy are decided by the Cabinet, which consists of some twenty members (the number is not fixed and invariable), but a number of senior ministers are not in the Cabinet and are invited to join in its deliberations only when a matter concerning the work of their own departments is involved. These ministers also are bound by Cabinet decisions and must refrain from opposing them. As soon as the Cabinet or a minister has decided upon a policy, the officials in his department, *i.e.* the civil servants, work out the details and, where necessary, prepare proposals to be put before Parliament.

The day-to-day work of the central government is, therefore, carried on by the civil servants, who are permanent officials holding their office "at the pleasure of the Crown". Unlike ministers they do not change when the government goes out of office, but are subject to rules of conduct designed to ensure loyalty to the minister at the head of their department at the time being. A civil servant disobeys those rules at his peril, for if he is disciplined for infringing them he has no redress in law since he holds his office at the discretion of the Crown. Membership of the Communist party, for example, might be held to be sufficient grounds for removal from office or transfer to another department, and higher civil servants are usually expected to abstain from taking an active part in national politics.

Each government department has a senior civil servant, known as the permanent secretary, at its head, who is responsible to the minister and his parliamentary secretary (a member of the government who is also a member of either the House of Lords or of the House of Commons). Under the permanent secretary are the deputy secretaries and then a hierarchy of administrative staff, including assistant secretaries, principals, assistant principals, and executive and clerical officers, as well as the various specialists.

Nationalised Industries

In addition to the major and minor government departments, the central machinery includes various national bodies which are not directly under a minister of the Crown and over which the control of Parliament is, therefore, limited. These include the boards controlling the nationalised industries, where a minister exercises general supervision over major policy, but is not concerned with day-to-day administration. The staffs of these boards are not civil servants holding office at the pleasure of the Crown, but are subject to the normal contractual relationship of employees in general. These national and semi-independent bodies operate usually by way of regional organisations throughout the country, and this also constitutes a new departure from the traditional pattern of central and local government.

Regional Organisations

Regional organisations, discussed experimentally before the Second World War, for example, during the General Strike of 1926, were introduced by the government as a wartime measure. As part of the Civil Defence organisation the country was divided into regions under Regional Commissioners, each of which could function independently if the central government was put out of action by enemy bombing or invasion. All government departments were represented in these Civil Defence Regions, which proved to be the pattern for a number of post-war developments, including the regional organisation of hospitals. This regional organisation has the advantage that the load of responsibility, and the benefits of the services, are distributed over a much wider area than that of the local authorities. The main disadvantage is that of remoteness from the people served. There is no doubt, however, that regionalisation has come to stay, but it does, in fact, mean that the pattern of local government is now overlaid in certain respects by an administrative machine which is not responsible to the local electors on the one hand, nor directly responsible to Parliament on the other.

Local Government

Local government is administered by two kinds of local authorities, major and minor. The major local authorities are the councils of the county boroughs and of the administrative counties. County boroughs are responsible for all services within their boundaries. The administrative counties are divided into county districts— urban and rural—administered by separate local councils. Rural districts are, in turn, divided into parishes (not to be confused with Church parishes), some of which have parish councils with limited administrative functions.

The term "on the parish" was used in the days when the parish was the unit of poor law relief, and it has a long history. The civil parishes were the original local government areas under the Elizabethan Poor Relief Act of 1601. The civil and ecclesiastical parishes were then the same, but in the course of time the number of ecclesiastical parishes was increased, while various statutes altered the boundaries of the civil parishes to make them conform to the county districts and county boundaries, and the powers of the "vestry" which governed a parish were steadily whittled away. The present position is, therefore, that urban parishes no longer have any local government responsibilities, and rural parish councils have only minor powers and duties. In general the main value of the rural parish organisation is that it serves as a means of ventilating local complaints.

The smallest effective units of local government are the county districts. These may be either urban or rural, and they spring from the sanitary districts set up under the Public Health Acts of the last century. Each district council consists of a chairman and councillors, elected for periods of three years. The chairman is elected annually by the councillors, and he is *ex officio* a justice of the peace for the county.

A district council is a body corporate with a common seal. Its functions are primarily concerned with sanitary matters. Each district council must employ a medical officer of health and a public health inspector (formerly known as a sanitary inspector), and appoint a clerk, a treasurer, and, in urban areas, a surveyor. Urban and rural district councils make and levy rates, and they may also act as the agents of the county councils for certain purposes.

With the growth of local government services, and the need to spread the load over wider areas, the administrative counties became increasingly important. An administrative county is not always the same as a geographical county. There is also a historical difference. When county councils were created, they assumed responsibility for the administrative work of the justices in quarter sessions and their boundaries followed the jurisdiction of the justices, including certain ancient franchises and liberties. It is for this reason that the three Ridings of Yorkshire, for example, all had separate county councils.

Each county council consists of county councillors directly elected by the local government electors, county aldermen elected by the councillors, and a chairman elected each year by the whole council. The chairman is also *ex officio* a justice of the peace for the county.

The chief officers of a county council are the clerk, who is usually also clerk of the peace, *i.e.* clerk to the justices in quarter sessions, the chief education officer, the county medical officer, the county treasurer, and the county surveyor. Specialist officers are also appointed under various statutes.

In contrast to the administrative counties, which date from 1888, the boroughs have a long and chequered history. Some have charters dating from ancient times, others were created for political reasons, and by the eighteenth century many had become corrupt, as witnessed by the adjectives "rotten" or "pocket", which were applied to them. The reform of the boroughs came in the 19th century when the legislature dissolved many of the small boroughs, and insisted on making the town councils conform to election by local government electors. In boroughs, the mayor, aldermen, and councillors form the council, the mayor having precedence as the first citizen. The chief officers of a municipal or county borough council are the town clerk, the medical officer of health, the borough treasurer, the surveyor, and other officers with special responsibilities, such as the education officer.

It will thus be seen that the machinery of government is a complex one, with central, regional, and local organisations, the last named being of both major and minor character. The system has many defects, and has received much attention of recent years, but it must be remembered that the golden thread running through all these services is the voluntary work of the members of the innumerable committees, advisory and executive.

CHAPTER IX

THE LEGISLATURE

The essence of a modern democracy is that those who control its destiny shall be answerable to the people for their actions. In Britain this is achieved by recognising that the Queen is the head of the State with the Government acting in her name, but the Government depends for its existence on the will of Parliament. This parliamentary supremacy was achieved only after many years of struggle, in the course of which the royal prerogative came to be exercised only through ministers answerable to Parliament.

In Tudor times, for example, Parliament was principally an instrument of the Crown for obtaining money and approving the actions of the king and his council. The monarch could, and often did, summon and dismiss a Parliament arbitrarily. The Stuart kings, and especially Charles I, carried this principle even further, and sometimes endeavoured to dispense with the summoning of Parliament for many years at a time. It was the reaction from this autocracy that led, through the Bill of Rights and the Act of Settlement, to the acceptance of the rule of the majority in Parliament, and the emergence of the three functions of government, *i.e.* legislative, executive, and judicial.

The executive functions are carried out by the Government, which can act, as already noted, only with the general approval of Parliament, and which derives its power mainly from Acts of Parliament. The legislative function is carried out by the legislature, which consists of the Queen in Council in Parliament. There are two Houses of Parliament, the House of Lords and the House of Commons, but the latter, the House of Commons, has been, in effect, the supreme legislative body since 1911, when the power of the House of Lords was drastically reduced.

The consent of the Queen is needed before any Act of Parliament can become law, but this is now a formality dependent on the principle that the prerogative of the Crown can be exercised only through ministers responsible to Parliament. Similarly, the powers of the House of Lords to reject measures already approved by the House of Commons is limited, for the Lords can delay the passage of a bill for only a certain length of time, and they have no power to reject a bill dealing with finance. A bill is the draft of a statute, and only when finally approved by the Queen does it become an effective Act of Parliament. The House of Lords has still a most important function in legislation, both as regards revising controversial measures and also as a means whereby bills not involving political controversy may be introduced to Parliament.

It is sometimes thought that Parliament is primarily concerned with legislation. This is not, in fact, the case. More than half of its time is devoted to acting as watchdog over the administration and to the remedying of grievances. It is this constant scrutiny of the executive which keeps ministers up to their work, and it is aided by the special privileges of members of Parliament, who are at liberty to raise any matter they please in the House without fear of subsequent legal action.

The early struggles for parliamentary supremacy turned primarily on the right to raise money by taxes. As soon as it was accepted that the consent of Parliament was required before taxation could be imposed the battle was half won. The matter was fought out by the Long Parliament and finally settled in the wording of the Bill of Rights: ". . . the levying of money for or to the use of the Crown by pretence of prerogative without grants of Parliament for longer time or in other manner than the same is or shall be granted is illegal". The next step was to break the power of the King to set aside Acts of Parliament by granting dispensations saying that they need not apply to certain people. James II was particularly prone to do this, and his actions led to the abolition of this dispensing power by the Bill of Rights.

At that time, and during the early part of the eighteenth century, the only way that a great minister of State could be coerced by Parliament was by the threat of impeachment, a lengthy and cumbersome process. It was not until Cabinet Government became effective that Parliament really gained full control. In the time of Queen Anne a confidential inner group of ministers, loosely known as the Cabinet, met under her presidency. When she died, her successor, George I, did not attend these meetings, and a Prime Minister presided in his place. From then onwards, party politics decided the leadership, often with the aid of bribery and "rigged" elections through the pocket boroughs and by other means. Thus it needed only parliamentary reform, through the Reform Act of 1832, to introduce a proper system of election by the people, at first the landowners, but later every adult male and female, to make the executive responsible to the will of the people through Parliament. Defeat on a major issue in the House of Commons means that a government must resign and give way to another.

The position now is, therefore, that Parliament can make, or unmake, any law that it wishes, and the validity of an Act of Parliament cannot be questioned, even by the courts of law. The latter can only interpret the statutes, they cannot alter them. Similarly, no Parliament can be bound by the Acts of an earlier Parliament, nor can it bind its successors. To do so would be to set limits to parliamentary supremacy. If it wished, Parliament could repeal all the statutes which have led to its supremacy and create a dictatorship, destroying itself in the process. Adverse decisions in the courts of law can be reversed by Parliament, if necessarily retrospectively. Indemnity Acts, making actions legal that were previously illegal, are good examples of parliamentary power. In practice, of course, Parliament does not enact statutes which cannot be enforced.

This matter of parliamentary supremacy is of the utmost importance in everyday life, for it may be the only safeguard the individual has against great authorities. Thus a ministry might become oppressively powerful, and claim that it derived its right to act in this manner from Parliament by delegation. The only body which could take away those powers by constitutional means would be Parliament itself. Another great safeguard is the respect which Parliament has always shown for the common law, for it is accepted that Parliament will not interfere with the rights of the subject to have access to the courts of law, and the courts, in turn, will have regard only to clear and unequivocal words in any Act of Parliament if these may be construed as an infringement of rights under the common law.

A third great safeguard is, of course, public opinion. No Parliament would dream of passing laws offensive to the mass of the people except in grave emergency. In line with this is the practice of consultation with any organisations that may be interested in, or affected by, new legislation. In a measure that would involve a section of industry, for example, Parliament would expect the responsible minister, through his department, to consult representatives of employers, the trade unions, and possibly research organisations. Similarly, a change of law involving local government would require consultation with representatives of the county councils and municipal corporations, and possibly also members of various voluntary organisations whose work might be involved. Parliament may, in its wisdom, expressly provide that a minister must not take action under a given statute unless he has conducted these enquiries, and satisfied himself that no hardship will result.

The House of Lords

The House of Lords is composed of the spiritual and temporal lords of Parliament. Put into plain language, this means that the Archbishops of Canterbury and York and the diocesan bishops of the Church of England form the lords spiritual, and the hereditary and life peers and certain judges make up the temporal peers.

The Archbishops of Canterbury and York, and the Bishops of London, Durham, and Winchester, sit in the House of Lords as of right. The remaining twenty-one spiritual lords are diocesan bishops sitting by right of seniority of date of appointment.

The temporal peers were formerly only the hereditary peers of the United Kingdom, together with certain representative Scottish and Irish peers. The creation of life peers, whose titles are not passed on to any successors, but lapse on the death of the holders, is a departure from tradition which is of great interest and importance.

As the House of Lords is also the supreme court of appeal in law, Lords of Appeal in Ordinary are appointed to carry out these judicial functions, and they hold office for life. Until recently, women were not allowed to sit in the House of Lords, but here, also, there has been a break with tradition with life peeresses now entitled to take their seats in Parliament. In practice the day-to-day work of the House of Lords is conducted by a relatively small number of peers, who attend regularly. Without a writ of summons for each Parliament a peer cannot take his seat in the House of Lords.

The House of Commons

The House of Commons, with members drawn from England, Scotland, Wales, and Northern Ireland, is elected by popular vote. Originally the franchise, or right to vote, was possessed only by males owning or occupying property of a certain value. This was gradually extended until in 1867 the artisan class, and many agricultural labourers, were given the right to vote provided that their lodgings had an annual value, unfurnished, of £10 per annum. At the end of the First World War the franchise was extended to all adult males and to women of thirty years of age, subject to certain qualifications. The present position is that all persons who have attained the age of twenty-one are entitled to have their names placed on the register of electors. They then have one vote in parliamentary elections, and one vote for each local government election. Certain persons, however, are disqualified from voting, even if their names do appear on the register. These include peers, infants (*i.e.* under twenty-one years of age), aliens (unless they have become naturalised), persons convicted of treason or felony (unless they have served their sentence or received a pardon). Persons convicted of corrupt and illegal practices at elections may not vote for five years.

The disqualifications for potential members of the House of Commons are more stringent. They include such categories as aliens, infants, the mentally disabled, peers, clergymen, bankrupts, and persons holding certain offices under the Crown. Anyone guilty of corrupt practices, and certain convicted persons, would also be disqualified from sitting or voting as a member of the House of Commons.

Over a long period of years it has become recognised that, because of their special position as servants of the Crown, it is essential that civil servants should be politically neutral, and the position is now that, in general, a civil servant wishing to seek election to the House of Commons must resign his office as soon as his intention to put himself forward as a candidate is announced.

Ministers of the Crown must, by convention, be members of one or other of the Houses of Parliament, and to make sure that there shall be representatives of the Government in both houses the number of ministers who may sit in the House of Commons is limited. It is, however, generally accepted that the principal government departments should be represented in the House of Commons, either by a minister or by his parliamentary secretary.

Members of the House of Commons cannot resign their seats, and they must submit themselves for re-election if they accept an office of profit under the Crown. Thus, a member wishing to resign accepts token office such as the Stewardship of the Chiltern Hundreds, or of the Manor of Northstead, and then fails to offer himself for re-election at the consequent by-election.

A new Parliament is summoned to meet by a royal proclamation, and it can be prorogued or dissolved only in the same manner. The Triennial Act of 1694 requires Parliament to meet at least every three years, but it must, in fact, meet at least once a year as the legislation authorising the raising and spending of public money is passed for only one year at a time.

After the Queen has proclaimed the calling together of a new Parliament, members of the House of Lords receive a writ of summons to attend. At the same time writs are issued to the returning officers, *i.e.* the sheriffs of counties, or mayors of parliamentary boroughs, commanding them to arrange for election of members of the House of Commons. Each candidate must be proposed and seconded by an elector, and his nomination paper must be signed by eight other electors. If more than one candidate is nominated for a vacancy a poll is ordered. Voting is by a secret ballot, in which each elector places a mark against the name of the candidate for whom he wishes to vote. The cost of an election is met out of public funds, but each candidate must be responsible for his own election expenses as these are not paid for by the State. In practice, the registration officers who maintain the register of voters, *i.e.* the clerks of the county councils and the town clerks of boroughs, do much of the work of the returning officers.

Each Parliament has a normal life of five years, and it is a convention of the constitution that the Queen will dissolve Parliament during this time only at the request of the Prime Minister. As noted earlier, a government defeat in the House of Commons on a major issue would result in its resignation or a request to the Queen by the Prime Minister to dissolve Parliament. In the event of the government resigning the Queen could ask the Leader of the Opposition to form a government, perhaps temporarily. Dissolution of Parliament automatically leads to a general election.

When a vacancy occurs in the House of Commons during its lifetime, it is the Speaker who authorises the issuing of a writ for a by-election, but the death of the reigning monarch no longer affects the duration of Parliament. A session of Parliament is terminated by prorogation, usually by a Commission under the Great Seal, and this puts an end to all the business, so that any bills which have not been completed must lapse. When prorogued, Parliament can be recalled at one day's notice if need be. The adjournment of Parliament is a domestic affair, to be decided by either House for as long as it wishes, and it does not put an end to parliamentary business.

A new session of Parliament is opened either by the Queen or by Royal Commissioners. Members of the House of Lords take the oath of allegiance immediately, but members of the House of Commons wait until they have chosen their Speaker and he has taken the oath. The first formal business is the speech from the Throne, usually delivered by the Queen in the House of Lords, or, if Parliament is opened by commission, by the Lord Chancellor. This speech outlines the government's plans for the session, and is the responsibility of the Cabinet. After it has been delivered an address is moved in answer to the speech, and a debate follows on the address, but there is first an echo of the early struggles of Parliament. Before this debate takes place each House asserts its ancient rights to consider matters not brought before it by the Crown (in other words, to redress the grievances of the country) by the formal reading of an obsolete bill dealing with "Select Vestries" in the Lords and "Clandestine Outlawries" in the Commons. The debate on the address then follows. In the House of Lords the formal proceedings are controlled by the Lord Chancellor, and in the House of Commons by the Speaker, but whereas the Speakers must be impartial, the Lord Chancellor may be a spokesman for the Government, in which case he steps aside from his seat on the woolsack.

When the House of Commons sits in committee, the chairman of the Committee of Ways and Means, or his deputy, takes the chair. These offices are party political appointments, but the holders do not take an active part in the debates in the House.

The Clerk of Parliaments in the House of Lords is appointed by the Crown, and can be removed from office only by the Crown. Under him are a Clerk Assistant and Reading Clerk appointed by the Lord Chancellor. The orders of the House of Lords are enforced by the Gentleman Usher of the Black Rod.

The Clerk of the House of Commons (the Under Clerk of the Parliaments) is appointed by the Crown, as are the two Clerk Assistants. The Sergeant-at-Arms enforces the orders of the House.

All proceedings of either House are public, except when held in secret session, and a verbatim report is published each day in the official *Parliamentary Debates* (*Hansard*).

Functions of Parliament

The main functions of Parliament are, firstly, to legislate, *i.e.* to make laws for regulating the conduct of the country; secondly, to provide for the appropriation of money and to make this available for the services provided by the State; and thirdly, to control the government in power.

Parliament retains the right to legislate on any matter it wishes, and only Parliament can authorise any other body to legislate. In former times, both government and opposition could initiate legislation, but with the growth of the political parties, and the complexity of the administrative requirements of the country, it is, in practice, the government that introduces almost all bills as a result of policy decisions made in the Cabinet. These decisions may, in turn, be instigated by the government departments that will be responsible for their administration when the bills finally become law.

A bill relating to some matter of local interest, or affecting some particular person or body of persons, including local authorities and statutory undertakings, such as water companies, may be dealt with as a private bill. A private bill must not be confused with a private member's bill, which is, in fact, a public bill introduced by a member of the House on his own initiative and on one of the days set apart for this purpose. There is no difference in procedure between a government bill and a private member's bill. Bills may be introduced into either House. Controversial political measures are dealt with first in the House of Commons, as being the more appropriate forum for this kind of discussion.

The process of passing a public bill is the same in both Houses. The bill is given a formal first reading on introduction. It is then printed and is given a second reading as a result of general debate. It is next referred to one of the standing committees appointed for the purpose, or, if it is sufficiently important, the whole House may resolve to sit in committee. During the committee stage various amendments are suggested, and incorporated into the bill if a majority of the committee so agrees. The bill is then reported to the House and debated further. It may, if deemed necessary, then be referred back to the committee. Finally, it is submitted for a third reading and, if passed, is sent from the Commons to the Lords, or from Lords to Commons, depending on its origin, and the same procedure begins again in the other House. The bill is finally sent to the Queen for the Royal Assent. This is given either in person or, usually, by commission. No bill has been vetoed by the Sovereign since the early eighteenth century.

Bills relating to the imposition or application of taxes must be introduced first in the House of Commons. It is for the Speaker of that House to decide whether a bill is a money bill within the meaning of the Parliament Act, 1911, which limited the powers of the Lords in several respects. If the Lords fail to pass, within one month, a bill passed by the Commons and endorsed by the Speaker as a money bill, or refuse to pass a public bill (other than a bill to extend the duration of Parliament) within a given period of time, it may be presented by the House of Commons to the Queen for approval.

Legislation authorising taxation and expenditure can be initiated only by a minister of the Crown, since its purpose is to provide money for the various services performed by the Crown. For this reason also, these bills, of which the most important are the Finance Bill, dealing with taxation, and the Appropriation Bill, which authorises expenditure, must be introduced first in the House of Commons on a resolution of a committee of the whole House. The House of Lords has no power in respect of money bills. This principle, that the Upper House must not interfere with the will of the people as shown through their elected representatives, also explains why a bill introduced by the Lords which is unacceptable to the Commons would never appear on the Statute Book, for the Commons would refuse to discuss it.

Much of the work of Parliament is done by committees, of which there are three kinds. There are the Standing Committees, composed of members of all political parties in proportion as they appear in the composition of the House of Commons, whose function is to examine in detail and amend the various Bills before these are presented to the whole House for further debate and a third reading. There are also certain official parliamentary committees, such as the Committee of Privileges, whose function is to act as watch-dog, on behalf of Parliament, to ensure that the freedom of members of Parliament is safeguarded, and the Select Committee on Estimates, which sees that public money is properly spent. The third group of committees is informal and *ad hoc*, set up to deal with particular issues of policy. It includes scientific committees as well as political party committees, and the influence of these committees on government policy may be quite considerable.

In addition to legislation, Parliament has the most important function of controlling the actions of the government. In matters of great moment this is done by passing a resolution of "no-confidence", or rejecting a proposal which the government has made an issue of "confidence". In either event, the government must resign.

Other measures of control include Question Time; one hour each day set aside during which members of Parliament may question any minister on matters for which he is responsible. These parliamentary questions and their answers are duly reported in the press, and serve a most valuable purpose in keeping the public informed. The House has the power to confirm or annul Orders and Regulations made by ministers, and the Opposition, or a group of members, can also force a debate on major issues of policy by adopting certain formalities of procedure.

The privileges of members of both Houses of Parliament have been hard-won over the centuries, and they are zealously guarded. They include freedom from arrest on a civil (but not a criminal) matter, freedom of speech, and the right to control their own proceedings, including the decision as to who shall be allowed to sit and vote. Both Houses have also the power to punish those who offend against them, even to the extent of commitment to prison.

Private Bills

A private bill is one relating to some particular place or a particular body of persons, for example, to give additional powers to one local authority or to a water company. After certain preliminary formalities, including advertisement of the objects of the bill, a printed copy must be deposited with Parliament by November 27th in any given year. There is, therefore, only one opportunity each year to promote a private bill. A private bill is given the most searching examination at the committee stage to determine whether or not there is any conflict between national and local interests. Promoters and opponents are represented by counsel, and the proceedings are quasi-judicial. If the bill is accepted in committee it is reported to the House and then proceeds in a similar manner to a public bill. The procedure is, therefore, costly and time-consuming, but it does permit local authorities to seek wider powers than would otherwise be practicable under public general Acts.

CHAPTER X
THE EXECUTIVE

The government of any country, or indeed the management of affairs in general, calls for the formulation of policy, and the implementing of this by administrative action. In Britain the executive power rests with the Crown, that is to say, with the Queen in Council, but the Sovereign entrusts this executive power to her ministers, who are, in turn, nominated by the leader of the political party that has a majority of votes in the House of Commons.

Until the eighteenth century the Privy Council was the chief source of executive power. With the development of the system of Cabinet government, the advisory and judicial functions of the Privy Council declined in importance, and its main work at the present time is the formal confirmation of policy decisions made elsewhere, usually by the Cabinet. The Privy Council is responsible for issuing Orders in Council, which are documents giving the force of law to important actions of the government. Members of the Privy Council are entitled to be known as "Right Honourable", and all take an oath of secrecy on appointment. The Judicial Committee of the Privy Council is the final court of appeal for certain legal matters arising within the British Commonwealth.

The Cabinet

Whereas the Privy Council is convened by the Clerk, whose office dates back some 400 years, the Cabinet is summoned by the Prime Minister. Both these terms require explanation. The Cabinet was originally the innermost circle of the Privy Council. To-day it consists of those ministers of the Crown who are invited by the Prime Minister to join him in advising the Queen on the government of the country. It was the Hanoverian kings, with their limited knowledge of the English language, who led to the present system of Cabinet government with a Prime Minister to act in their absence. The Cabinet has no statute or rule of common law to support it, and its existence rests on convention. The office of Prime Minister is also conventional, for it is not defined by statute or rule of common law either, and his official title is First Lord of the Treasury. It was not until 1905 that the office of Prime Minister, which had been in existence for nearly 200 years, was officially recognised, and its holder given precedence as the fourth person in the realm after the Royal Family.

It is the duty of the Prime Minister to keep the Queen informed of the business of the government, to preside over the Cabinet, to supervise the various government departments, and to answer to Parliament for all actions of the government. In addition, he is responsible for recommending the appointment of many high dignitaries, such as archbishops, bishops, the Lord Chief Justice, and lords lieutenant of counties. He is also responsible for recommending the award of civil honours and distinctions.

The Prime Minister selects the Cabinet ministers, but no minister can claim a seat by virtue of his office. There is, however, a convention that certain Officers of State, such as the Lord Chancellor, the Chancellor of the Exchequer, and certain ministers in charge of large and important departments, shall have a seat in the Cabinet.

The purpose of the Cabinet is to formulate government policy and to co-ordinate and control the various activities of the State. Cabinet meetings are private, and the proceedings are strictly confidential, the members being bound by their oath as Privy Councillors, and also by the Official Secrets Acts forbidding the publication of State papers. Ministers not in the Cabinet are called to attend when matters affecting their departments are discussed, and they may also be members of Cabinet committees. Records are kept by the Cabinet Office, or Secretariat of the Cabinet, which is also responsible for providing information and advice for ministers, and for issuing the directives and decisions of the Prime Minister and the Cabinet to the various government departments concerned. The Cabinet Office is therefore of the utmost importance both in peace and in war.

One of the administrative problems confronting the central government is that of co-ordination. Here the various Cabinet committees play an essential part, for they can dispose of business not important enough to come before the full Cabinet. They also focus issues sharply before these are presented to the Cabinet for decision. In essence, the Cabinet, or a ministerial committee, decides on policy after considering the advice of its experts, and the government department concerned then takes the necessary action. The composition of Cabinet committees is never disclosed, in case the principle of the collective responsibility of the Cabinet for its actions should be weakened.

The term "ministerial responsibility" embraces the collective responsibility of the Government as a whole for its policy and actions, together with the responsibility of each minister to Parliament for the work of his department. Any minister who finds himself unable to agree with his colleagues must resign. If a minister is criticised adversely in Parliament for some action by his department, he may find himself supported by the Cabinet, which then accepts the matter as one of confidence in the government. On the other hand, the Cabinet may disown him, when he must stand or fall alone, even to the extent of losing his office.

The present system of central government is the outcome of government by party, dating from the latter part of the reign of Charles II when the Whigs and Tories (later to become Liberals and Conservatives) became the principal opponents in Parliament. Labour candidates for Parliament first appeared in 1892, and the Labour Party was formed from the Labour Representative Committee in 1906. In both Houses attendance of members on important occasions is secured by officials known as whips (originally whippers-in), who issue circular letters known as a "whip". Failure to respond to an urgent whip is regarded as a very grave matter by the party concerned.

The Civil Service

Ministers are assisted in their work by the permanent officials of the civil service, which is divided into various classes. There is no comprehensive legal or statutory definition of a civil servant, for his employment and status are governed rather by traditional practice, agreements, and regulations, than by statute. It is, however, generally accepted that a practical working definition to the effect that a civil servant is a servant of the Crown employed in a civil capacity and paid wholly and directly out of moneys voted by Parliament meets the case. Holders of political or judicial office do not come within the categories of civil servants.

Under this wide definition are included many industrial employees, and the term "civil servant" is customarily confined to the non-industrial staffs of the various government departments. The employees of public corporations and of nationalised industries are not civil servants.

It should be remembered that the civil servant differs from an ordinary employee in two important respects. Firstly, as a servant of the Crown, he holds his office and related privileges, such as a pension, as a matter of grace and not of right. Secondly, the principle of collective responsibility within the government means that the civil servant must always consider the effects of his actions in the light that he should under no circumstances act in a way that would commit or embarrass the minister to whom he is responsible.

The nature of his work is such that the civil servant must be prepared to accept restrictions which do not apply to the ordinary man. He may, for example, take part in political activities only by permission, and subject to certain conditions, for it is his duty to serve the government to the best of his ability without regard to his private political views. Similarly, his private activities must not conflict with his official duties, and he must pay especial attention to the Official Secrets Acts and to the Prevention of Corruption Acts. As it would be most improper for a civil servant to use his official position to further his own ends, he must, as a general rule, refrain from engaging in business and commerce, and he must certainly not develop any personal interests in public contracts. Information gained in his official capacity may not be used in writing books or articles, or in broadcasts or lectures, without the prior and express approval of his seniors within the department in which he works. In the same way, inventions by civil servants may be subject to strict rules.

These restrictions vary according to the responsibilities of the officer concerned. In the industrial, minor and manipulative, and messengerial classes, there are no restrictions on political activities, except that a serving civil servant cannot sit in the House of Commons. Candidates for election must, therefore, resign before nomination day. Senior civil servants, *e.g.* those in the administrative class, are debarred from national political activities, but may engage in local government if they obtain permission to do so. The intermediate grades of civil servants must generally obtain permission before engaging in political activities. In view of the vital importance of secrecy in matters affecting the security of the State, anyone whose reliability is in doubt cannot be employed on confidential work. Although, therefore, the government does not normally concern itself with the private political complexion of its servants, the membership of certain organisations would be considered a grave matter for people concerned in security aspects of the work.

On the other hand, there are privileges attaching to the office of civil servant, for the minister assumes responsibility for the faults of his department, and the Treasury will, as a matter of grace, undertake the defence of law suits in which officers may become involved in consequence of carrying out their official duties. In effect, therefore, while a servant of the Crown holds office at the pleasure of the Crown, and may be dismissed without the remedy of appeal to the courts, his tenure is secure, for a permanent official is dismissed only for serious misconduct, and after the most searching enquiries. That is as it should be, for entry to the civil service is now possible only after the most meticulous scrutiny of personal and educational qualifications. It was not always so. Until about 100 years ago recruitment was by patronage and political influence, each department chose its own staff, and there were no standards of qualification.

In 1854, Sir Stafford Northcote and Sir Charles Trevelyan produced their Report on the Organisation of the Permanent Civil Service, in which they recommended the substitution of open competition in place of appointment by purchase or personal influence. They also advised that an independent body, the Civil Service Commission, should be established to organise recruitment to the service.

This Commission came into existence in 1855. The Commissioners are appointed, and their powers and duties are regulated, by Order in Council. Administratively, the Commission is a subordinate department of the Treasury, but in the selection of entrants to the civil service it is independent of ministerial or parliamentary control. It is also the duty of the Commissioners to study the careers of those selected in order to ensure that the methods of recruitment are in keeping with the requirements of the service, and with the level of education in the schools and universities.

Although the system of open competition dates from 1855, it was not until 1870 that it was made applicable to all appointments agreed upon by the Treasury, the department concerned, and the Commissioners. Fixed rules were then made, but power was retained to depart from these in special cases. The present position is that established appointments are now subject to the issue of a certificate of fitness from the Civil Service Commissioners to the effect that the candidate has been found to be suitably qualified in age, health, character, knowledge, and general ability. Some specialists whose qualifications and ability are already known, and of whose services the government has need, may be recruited without examination, but here, also, enquiries into health and personal standards may be made.

The undisputedly high standard of integrity of the civil service is, in the main, the product of this searching examination on entry, but there is also the important factor of central control of the service as a whole by the Treasury. One of the Joint Permanent Secretaries to the Treasury is the official head of the civil service, and also principal adviser to the Prime Minister on all matters concerning it. The Treasury circulars and minutes to the permanent heads of departments supplement the Orders in Council by which the civil service is regulated, and Treasury control extends to salaries and conditions of employment, the numbers of staffs, and the creation of higher posts.

Pattern of Staff Organisation

Although the number of government departments has multiplied greatly in the present century, the pattern of organisation is similar in each one. At the head is the Permanent Secretary, known as the Permanent Under-Secretary of State in those departments where the minister is a Secretary of State, for example, in the Home Office and the Foreign Office. He is assisted by one or more deputy secretaries, who have, in turn, under-secretaries and assistant secretaries. There is also a principal finance officer, a director or principal of the establishment and organisation division, and various specialist officers and professional advisers, such as the solicitor or legal adviser, and the chief medical officer. Many departments have their own statistical and information divisions or branches. The various classes of civil servants fit in with this general pattern of organisation.

The administrative class is recruited mainly from university graduates, and it is responsible for advising the minister on policy, including the possible difficulties of implementing new measures, in addition to dealing with problems arising in the execution of existing policy. The new entrant usually begins his career as an assistant principal, and then proceeds by way of principal to assistant secretary.

The executive class is responsible for the day-to-day conduct of the business of the departments within the defined limits of policy, including supply, contracts, and accounts. Recruitment is either by competitive examination from school at age eighteen or nineteen, or at a later age by selection and promotion from within the service. Executive officers begin as junior executive officers, and then proceed to higher executive officers, and finally to senior executive officers. It is practicable for an executive officer to achieve promotion to the higher administrative posts, or to train for special work.

The clerical class is usually recruited either from school at age sixteen or seventeen, or by promotion from within the service, after competitive examination. This class is responsible for general clerical work—checking, filing, record keeping, accounts, and the preparation of documents for senior officers.

In addition to the classes already mentioned there are several others, for example, the professional, scientific, and technical classes, including doctors, lawyers, engineers, and research workers. These officers may undertake advisory and inspectorial duties, and under certain circumstances they are also responsible for a considerable amount of administration.

Special groups of civil servants are found in certain departments, for example, the tax inspectors of the Board of Inland Revenue, the factory inspectors of the Ministry of Labour, and the Water-guard of the Department of Customs and Excise.

The Foreign Service is separately organised. All members are liable for service at home and abroad and for any type of work, including the diplomatic and consular service, and commercial and information services. At many overseas posts part of the staffs are recruited locally on a temporary basis, and are not eligible for pensions.

Civil servants may also be divided into those who are established and those who are unestablished. The former are permanent civil servants with security of tenure of service to the age of sixty, when they may be retired on pension, or asked to continue on a yearly basis to sixty-five. In very exceptional circumstances extensions beyond this age may be allowed. Pensions, which are a matter of grace and not of right, are of the non-contributory variety, and vary according to the length of service. Unestablished officers, although known as temporary officers, may be "permanent" in the sense that they may work until the normal retiring age, when they may be granted a gratuity but not a pension. They may also have the same privileges as their established colleagues with regard to annual leave, sick leave, and travelling and subsistence allowances, but temporary civil servants have no security of tenure.

All new entrants to the permanent civil service serve a period of probation lasting from one to two years, and promotions are made by the departments concerned, either following examination or by selection. All promotions to the administrative class, however, require Treasury approval, and appointments to the highest posts must be approved by the Prime Minister. Government departments must, of necessity, vary in their administrative structure according to the nature of their work, but, in general, there are divisions and branches for the various kinds of administration. It is the practice in many departments to transfer young officers from one branch of work to another to gain experience. There are also various methods of securing further training after entry into the service, by means of "refresher" courses and special leave schemes.

One of the most important characteristics of the civil service is its non-political character. This dates, in part, from the parliamentary reforms of the eighteenth and early nineteenth centuries, in addition to the innovations recommended by Northcote and Trevelyan in 1854. Their scheme, for central recruitment by open competition, paved the way for a unified service so that increasing demands could be met, as required, by the interchange of trained civil servants between one department and another. In turn, this unification ensured a continuity of experience far exceeding that possessed by any single individual, and this collective administrative experience is of the utmost value to the government when deciding on questions of policy. As Sir Edward Bridges said in his Rede Lecture to the University of Cambridge in 1950, entitled *Portrait of a Profession,* "it is a cardinal feature of British administration that no attempt should be made to formulate a new policy without the fullest consultation with those who have the practical experience in that field, and with those who will be called upon to carry it out".

The last century has witnessed the evolution of the civil servant from an individual appointed by patronage, and owing allegiance only to the minister who secured his place for him, to a highly educated member of a service renowned for its integrity and freedom from political bias. This process of evolution is likely to continue during the coming years, both by reason of the increasing complexity of government administration and also because the work of the civil servant, the employee of the public corporations and the nationalised industries, the private industrialist, and the trade union official, to mention only a few, will overlap to an increasing degree.

The modern state cannot survive in a fiercely competitive world unless its administrative machine is able to adjust rapidly and efficiently to changing needs and circumstances. It is possible, indeed probable, that the men and women who tend that machine will require to be experienced in the techniques and economics of industry, as well as in the art of administration. That tendency is already evident in the universities whence many of the higher civil servants are drawn, for courses in the basic sciences are becoming increasingly available to members of the arts faculties. The civil service will undoubtedly offer careers of great interest to young men and women in the future, both on the technical and administrative sides.

CHAPTER XI

THE JUDICIARY

The control exercised by Parliament over the central and local government administration is, in theory, unlimited, since the supremacy of Parliament enables it to make new laws, or abolish old ones, as it may think fit. Government departments, also, can influence policy, subject to parliamentary control, and local government authorities can operate within the powers conferred by the statutes. It is now necessary to consider the control exerted by the courts of law.

The primary function of the judiciary is to hear and determine disputes, either between individuals, or between individuals and the State. In so doing, the judges are bound by the common law of the land, and by the decisions of Parliament as expressed in the statutes. In reaching their decisions, however, by way of cases already decided, i.e. case law, and the interpretation of the statutes, they may make new law, as well as applying the existing law.

This function is of great importance, for it ensures that parliamentary supremacy, i.e. the will of the people of the realm as expressed through their elected representatives, can be enforced where necessary by the courts. It also means that the judges, in their interpretation of the law, can clarify obscurities, rectify abuses, and modify the statute laws so that they do not bear harshly or unjustly on the individual case or person before them.

There is no written code of laws in Britain, and each case must be decided by the judges on the evidence set before them. In reaching a decision attention will be paid to the common law, to the statutes, and also to the opinions expressed by learned judges in similar cases in the past. Attention may also be paid to the views expressed by academic lawyers in their writings on the subject under consideration.

The common law is of great antiquity, having been built up slowly by the decisions of the courts over many centuries. As the common law crystallised, harshness became apparent, and another system of law known as equity came into existence based on conscience and the protection of the rights of the individual. For a considerable time two sets of courts existed side by side, one applying the principles of the common law and the other those of equity, but in 1873 these courts were fused, so that all now apply similar rules, but if there is a conflict between the ancient common law and the principles of equity, then equity prevails.

Many of the principles of the common law have come to be embodied in the statutes, and administration is now governed largely by statute law, which includes not only the Acts of Parliament itself, but also subordinate legislation, such as statutory rules and orders, made by ministers under powers conferred on them by Parliament.

Courts of Law

The courts of law are broadly divisible into civil courts and criminal courts, but there is no hard and fast distinction between the two. They may best be described in the ascending order of importance, beginning with criminal offences.

Justices of the peace, or magistrates, are appointed by the Crown on the advice of the Lord Chancellor. These men and women are not paid for their services and their responsibilities are now mainly judicial, although a few administrative duties remain from former times. Two or more justices may form a court of petty sessions, where minor offences are dealt with. More serious offences may be tried in these courts if the accused so wishes and the magistrates agree. Petty sessional courts also conduct preliminary enquiries into indictable offences to determine whether or not the accused shall be committed for trial.

Appeal from a decision of a court of petty sessions lies to the justices of the whole county sitting in quarter sessions. Nearly all county courts of quarter sessions are presided over by a chairman or deputy-chairman who is a barrister or solicitor of ten years' standing, and to whom a salary may be paid. Borough courts of quarter sessions are presided over by a Recorder, a practising barrister appointed by the Crown and paid, out of borough funds, a salary prescribed by the Crown. The Recorder sits with a jury. From quarter sessions appeal lies on a point of law, by means of a case stated at the request of the defendant or of the prosecution, to the Queen's Bench Division of the High Court. A case may be stated by justices in petty sessions without a preliminary appeal to quarter sessions. These appeals are heard by a divisional court of three judges of the Queen's Bench Division. (Note: the term "Queen's Bench" or "King's Bench" is used according to whether the reigning monarch is a Queen or a King.)

Lay justices have been criticised as being sometimes too much in the hands of their clerk, or too willing to accept police evidence. In the Metropolitan Police District of London the courts are presided over by stipendiary magistrates, and many provincial towns also have stipendiary magistrates. In 1948 a Royal Commission (Cmd 7643, 1948, H.M.S.O.) expressed the view that the substitution of stipendiary magistrates for unpaid justices would involve great expense, and also lose the appreciation of laymen with the law.

The more serious crimes are known as indictable offences because a formal written accusation, or indictment, is required for their prosecution. These indictable crimes are tried with a jury at quarter sessions, the assizes, or the Central Criminal Court. Certain offences are excluded from the jurisdiction of quarter sessions, *e.g.* treason, murder, offences (other than burglary) punishable with life imprisonment, and also offences likely to involve difficult questions of law. A limited class of indictable offences may be dealt with summarily if the accused consents to this procedure.

Juvenile courts are special magistrates' courts for the trial of young offenders charged with any offence except homicide. Juvenile courts deal also with children in need of care and protection, or who are beyond the control of their parents, and with many of the applications for the adoption of children. A juvenile court consists of not more than three justices drawn from a special panel, and the general public is excluded from the hearing. Similarly, the hearing of domestic proceedings is separated from other business and heard by not more than three magistrates, one of whom must be a man and one a woman, the general public being excluded here also.

Courts of assize are branches of the High Court of Justice, and criminal cases are tried by jury before a High Court judge, or a Commissioner of Assize who may be a barrister commissioned to act as a judge. The assize judges work on the circuits into which England and Wales are divided, and travel from one county town to another. Assizes are normally held three times a year in each county, and in certain large cities which have their own assizes.

Any indictable offence committed within the county may be tried at assizes, and at the winter and summer assizes civil business is taken as well as criminal. Assize judges have the unlimited jurisdiction of the High Court in dealing with civil cases, but very rarely exercise the jurisdiction of the Chancery Division. Similarly, Divorce, but not Probate or Admiralty, jurisdiction is exercised at assizes. The autumn assize is confined to criminal cases, except in a few large towns.

Under the Criminal Justice Administration Act of 1956, Crown courts were established at Liverpool and Manchester to act as courts of assize for the area and also as courts of quarter sessions for those cities. These courts are presided over by the Recorder of Liverpool and the Recorder of Manchester.

The Central Criminal Court at the Old Bailey, in London, acts as the court of assize for criminal business for London. The Queen's Bench Division of the High Court also possesses criminal jurisdiction dating from ancient times, but this is now exercised only in a supervisory capacity, *e.g.* to ensure that a fair trial may be secured where there is much local prejudice the Queen's Bench division may direct that a case be tried elsewhere than in the court which would have had jurisdiction.

From assizes and quarter sessions, an appeal lies against conviction or sentence to the Criminal Division of the Court of Appeal. Appeals on questions of law may be brought as of right, but otherwise only by leave of the court or the trial judge. The court is composed of the Lord Chief Justice and the judges of the Queen's Bench Division, and usually consists of three judges, which is the minimum number required by statute. A single judgment is delivered, and appeal lies to the House of Lords if a point of law of general public importance is involved.

County courts are the chief lower courts for the trial of civil disputes. Some matters are placed specifically within the jurisdiction of the county court by statute or ministerial order. They are presided over by a county court judge, who must be a barrister of at least seven years' standing before being appointed. He usually sits alone, although he may sit with a jury, *e.g.* when fraud is alleged, or in the trial of certain actions, such as defamation, remitted from the High Court. The county courts are not in continuous session, so that one judge presides over several courts.

The High Court

Civil cases which lie outside the jurisdiction of the county courts are heard in High Court of Justice. Before the year 1875, there was a number of superior courts. They included the three Common Law Courts, *i.e.* the Court of King's Bench, which was originally concerned with offences against the King's Peace, the Court of Common Pleas to decide matters between the King's subjects, and the Court of Exchequer dealing with the revenues of the Crown. The other High Courts included the Court of Chancery, dealing with equity under the jurisdiction of the Lord Chancellor, the Admiralty Court, the Court of Probate, and the Court of Divorce and Matrimonial Causes.

Under the Judicature Act of 1873 all these courts, together with the courts of assize, were amalgamated into the Supreme Court of Judicature, consisting of the High Court of Justice and the Court of Appeal. The High Court of Justice sits in three divisions: the Queen's Bench Division, the Chancery Division, and the Probate,

Divorce, and Admiralty Division. The judges of the High Court are the Lord Chancellor, the Lord Chief Justice, the Master of the Rolls, and a number of judges without special office of their own and known, therefore, as puisne judges.

The Queen's Bench Division is concerned mainly with every kind of common law action, for it exercises the jurisdiction of the three Common Law Courts mentioned above. In addition, it has criminal jurisdiction, and has the power to supervise inferior courts and other judicial bodies by authority derived from the ancient prerogative writs of *mandamus*, commanding a person or body to do his or its duty, *certiorari* to remove a case from an inferior court into the High Court, and *prohibition*, to prevent an inferior court from exceeding its jurisdiction, or acting contrary to the rules of natural justice. These writs have now been replaced by orders with the same titles, and *mandamus*, for example, can be used to compel a government department to perform a public duty which has been laid upon it by statute. Similarly, an order of *prohibition* will operate to restrain ministers of the Crown and public authorities when they are acting in a "judicial" capacity, in the wide sense of imposing obligations on others.

The Chancery Division derives from the old Court of Chancery in which equity, originally intended to deal with cases in which the common law operated harshly, or gave no remedy at all, had developed a number of remedies, such as injunction and specific performance, and the law relating to trusts. Nowadays, the rules of equity may be applied by any judge in any division of the High Court, but the Chancery Division continues to deal with cases formerly dealt with in courts of equity, viz. partnerships, trusts, mortgages, the specific performance of contracts, the administration of estates of deceased persons and those of infants, and company and bankruptcy matters. The Lord Chancellor is the nominal head of this division, but the work is, in fact, done by the puisne judges.

The work undertaken by the Probate, Divorce, and Admiralty Division is apparent from its name. Probate relates to the proving of wills and letters of administration. Divorce jurisdiction in undefended cases has also been given to Commissioners in London and in the provinces, where local county court judges are generally appointed to act in this capacity. Matters of probate and divorce were originally dealt with by the ecclesiastical courts, and the influence of the ancient Roman law is strong in this division of the High Court. Admiralty business is concerned with shipping cases, and particularly with collisions at sea.

Appeal Courts

The courts of appeal in civil law actions are the Court of Appeal and the House of Lords. The Court of Appeal forms part of the Supreme Court of Judicature, and the normal membership of the Court is composed of the Master of the Rolls and the Lords Justices of Appeal. The Court sits in divisions, with three judges in each division.

The House of Lords is the supreme court of appeal, and in it is vested the ancient jurisdiction of the High Court of Parliament. Appeal lies from the Court of Appeal, with the leave of the House of Lords or of the Court of Appeal. The sittings are, traditionally, the ordinary sessions of the House of Lords, but in practice no lay peer has taken part in hearing an appeal since O'Connell's case in 1844.

Appeals are usually heard by five of the Lords of Appeal in Ordinary, who are salaried judges holding peerages for life. The other Law Lords who are entitled to sit are the Lord Chancellor, ex-Lord Chancellors, and any peers who have held high judicial office. The House of Lords is bound by its own decisions and an appeal is either allowed or dismissed, the result being entered in the Journals of the House. A member of the Court who dissents expresses his opinion, which is recorded. As already noted, appeals from the Criminal Division of the Court of Appeal can be brought only on a point of law of general public importance.

Special Courts

In addition to the courts already mentioned there are various special courts, such as those of Coroners, the Ecclesiastical Courts, and also administrative tribunals exercising judicial functions.

The office of coroner is of ancient origin, and his duties include the holding of enquiries into sudden, violent, or unnatural deaths. This he may do by holding an inquest in court, and he must do so, with a jury, if he has reason to believe that the death resulted from murder, manslaughter, infanticide, an accident involving a vehicle on the public highway, and in certain other special circumstances. If the jury returns a verdict of murder, manslaughter, or infanticide, the coroner commits the person concerned for trial at assizes. It is also the coroner's duty to hold an inquest to decide whether gold or silver objects found, and the owner of which cannot be traced, are treasure trove. Although treasure trove rests in the Crown, the finder receives the objects back or is paid their full market value. Coroners must be barristers, solicitors, or legally qualified medical practitioners, of not less than five years' standing.

They are appointed and paid by the county or county borough councils.

Ecclesiastical courts now have jurisdiction only in ecclesiastical matters. Although the hierarchy of courts still exists, the Court of the Archdeacon is almost obsolete. The Consistory Court, the principal ecclesiastical court of a diocese, has as judge the chancellor of the diocese, who is usually a barrister and appointed by the bishop.

Although all courts of law are the Queen's Courts, and derive their jurisdiction directly or indirectly from the Crown, the right of the monarch to deliver justice in person was finally disposed of in the *Prohibitions del Roy* of 1607, when all the judges, led by Chief Justice Coke, ruled that King James I could not adjudge any case in his own person. With the victory of Parliament in the constitutional struggles with the Stuart Kings the right of the Crown to create any new courts to administer any system of law, except the common law, without Parliamentary approval was also lost. This is of great importance in view of the growth of administrative tribunals in recent times. The third step, to secure the independence of the judges, came with the Act of Settlement of 1701. Hitherto, judges had held office at the royal pleasure, but now it was decreed that they should hold office during good behaviour, that their salaries should be fixed, and that they should be removed from office by the Sovereign only "upon an address of both Houses of Parliament". Only once since 1701 has such an address been moved, and this was against a judge convicted of misappropriation of funds in 1830.

The present position is, therefore, that all judges, from the law lords to the justices of the peace, are free to administer the law impartially without fear of pressure from the executive or from the legislature. If, in the course of interpreting the meaning of a statute, the courts reached a decision contrary to the intention and policy of the government, the remedy would be for Parliament to pass an amending Act or to make a new statute.

Central responsibility for the administration of the machinery of justice rests in part with the Lord Chancellor, and in part with the Home Secretary, for there is no separate office of Minister of Justice.

Although magistrates courts are independent and can be controlled judicially only by the Queen's Bench Division of the High Court by way of prerogative orders, the Home Secretary is responsible for their general administration, and, in the interests of uniformity, he issues advisory circulars on such matters as sentences, fines, and the interpretation of statutes and regulations. The Home

Secretary is also responsible *inter alia* for the probation system and the care of juvenile delinquents, for the administration of prisons through the Prison Commission, and for Borstal and other institutions for young offenders.

Judicial Problems

It is customary to divide the three functions of government into legislative, executive, and judicial, and the boundaries between them are, of necessity, ill-defined. When the exercise of a power lies on the border-line between the judicial and executive functions, *i.e.* when the action required to be taken is partly administrative and partly judicial, the process may be described as "quasi-judicial", as, for example, when a ministry official holds a public enquiry into the making of an order by a local authority, and the minister subsequently confirms or rejects the order.

It is in this field of quasi-judicial functions that difficulty commonly arises. If too much power is delegated to ministers parliamentary supremacy is weakened. If the judges cannot control the adjudication their independence of action in exercising their functions becomes useless. On the other hand, rigid supervision by the legislature or the judicature, or both, would make it difficult for administrative measures to be sufficiently flexible to work efficiently, for the administrator must act, or initiate action, and he cannot wait, as the judge does, until a dispute arises which requires settling. Ministers may be given absolute discretion by Parliament, and in such cases the only challenge in law can be whether the minister acted within the powers of the statute or regulation. Otherwise, he would be answerable only to Parliament for his actions.

More commonly, discretionary powers are not absolute, and provision is made in the statute for an appeal to the courts. In such cases, the courts may enquire whether or not the administrator is exceeding his statutory powers, *i.e.* acting *ultra vires,* and also whether the powers conferred by statute have been wrongly or improperly used. As the matter may also be raised in Parliament there is then, in effect, a double check on the use of statutory power by ministers and their departments.

When Parliament has expressly approved a course of action, those who carry it out must, in law, be right, provided that they do not exceed, or abuse, their powers by doing something for a wrong purpose, or in the wrong way. The rules of natural justice must be observed, and the person concerned must act in good faith. Similarly, excessive expenditure may be illegal, even with a lawful objective. The rules of natural justice are clear and simple. Both sides must be heard, no man can be a judge in his own cause, and there must be no bias. As was pointed out in Dr Bentley's case, decided in 1723: "Even God Himself did not pass sentence upon Adam before he was called upon to make his defence. 'Adam,' says God, 'where art thou? Hast thou not eaten of the tree that thou shouldst not eat?'" These principles have crystallised in the maxim that "Justice should not only be done, but should manifestly and undoubtedly be seen to be done".

The Committee on Ministers' Powers recommended in 1932 that when a minister acted in a judicial or quasi-judicial capacity, the reasons for the decision should be made known to the parties concerned, and also that the report of an inspector holding an enquiry should be made available to the parties heard. Neither of these proposals has been accepted as a rule of law, for there are practical difficulties, but it is generally accepted that any administrator or administrative tribunal must pay regard to the principles involved.

By-laws made by subordinate bodies, under powers delegated by Parliament or a minister, may be declared invalid either because they are *ultra vires*, or because they are oppressive or unreasonable. It goes without saying that, if an order by a minister conflicts with the Act which sanctions it being made, the courts will insist that the order must give way to the Act. If Parliament wishes to exclude the jurisdiction of the courts it must say so specifically in some such terms as "and shall not be questioned in any legal proceedings whatsoever". In general, however, no government would wish, except in times of grave emergency, to act in this manner. Administrative tribunals are intended to be conducted on the same principles of fairness and impartiality as are the proceedings of the courts of law.

Administrative Tribunals

One inevitable result of delegation of administrative work by Parliament to ministers has been an increase in the number of administrative tribunals. That is particularly so in the field of social services. The acquisition of land, slum clearance, national insurance, and national medical services, for example, require some machinery for enquiry into the facts of a dispute, and for an administrative decision to be made in accordance with established policy. Many of these issues are not of a kind suitable for reference to courts of law, which are not concerned with policy.

Apart from this, the formal machinery of the law is costly to operate and relatively slow in action, and the judges are bound by rules of law in interpreting the statutes. On the other hand, the traditional legal system, with its judges completely independent and administering the law openly and publicly, arose partly because of the manifest failings of the early and secret administrative tribunals, such as the Court of Star Chamber. Members of a tribunal, dependent on a minister for their re-appointment, might reasonably be expected to regard him with considerable respect, particularly if their appointment was a salaried one. In some tribunals, representation of the parties by a professional lawyer is expressly excluded, and in others the chairman may not necessarily have any legal experience, so that there is the danger of minor considerations being given more weight than they would receive in a law court. Tribunals need not follow precedent, nor need they publish reasons for their decision. The question of appeal from an adverse decision is also a difficult one. Sometimes there is no appeal, and in other cases an appeal lies to the minister or to another tribunal appointed by him. In some instances the full range of appeal in law is allowed, *i.e.* to the High Court, to the Court of Appeal, and to the House of Lords.

The tribunal system has evolved piecemeal, and its further development needs to be watched with care. Fortunately it is in the interest of the country as a whole, and not least of the ministers most closely concerned, to ensure that the essential requirements of justice are observed.

Tribunals are of various kinds, and classification is difficult. Generally speaking, however, they may be divided into three broad categories. There are statutory tribunals to enforce professional discipline, such as the Disciplinary Committees of the General Medical Council and of the Law Society. Other tribunals are concerned especially with disputes involving government departments or public authorities, such as pensions appeals tribunals, and there is the large group of tribunals where specialised knowledge is required of the members by reason of the nature of the disputes to be settled, as, for example, rents tribunals, and those concerned with the fixing of fares, freight rates, and the granting of licences.

CHAPTER XII

LOCAL GOVERNMENT

The long history of local government brings out well the struggles to retain local freedom of action, and to avert the imposition of strong central control.

In the early Middle Ages, each English shire or county had its own assembly for judicial and administrative purposes. Within the shire were the courts of the hundreds, the manors, and the boroughs possessing Royal Charters. From the time of Henry II the royal judges, the justices in eyre, began increasingly to control, and later supersede, these local courts, by means of the circuits of assize and gaol delivery. Reference has already been made to the creation of justices of the peace in the fourteenth century, and their combination of judicial and administrative duties. When the powers of the King in Council were curtailed and the Court of Star Chamber abolished, central control was much diminished. Instead, in the eighteenth century, Parliament resorted to the creation of independent bodies for special services, but it is a far cry from the inefficient and often corrupt administration of the eighteenth and early nineteenth centuries to local government of the present day by elected representatives.

Although local authorities were reformed, and the process of democratic election assured, Parliament continued to establish *ad hoc* authorities, *e.g.* the school boards under the Education Act of 1870, over which central control could be maintained, and it was not until the present century that the all-purposes local authority could be said to be fully developed.

It is interesting to see how the pendulum is now tending to swing in the direction of greater delegation of responsibility by counties under schemes of divisional administration or direct delegation of functions. As will appear, central control remains, but in a less obtrusive form than in past centuries.

Up to the onset of the Second World War, more and more responsibility was placed on local authorities, and especially the counties and county boroughs, mainly as a result of the rapid development of social services. Since that war some have been transferred to statutory bodies, operating usually on a regional basis, or to government departments. On the other hand, the National Health Service Act increased the burden of the county and county borough councils by giving them the title of Local Health Authorities, with additional duties in the prevention of disease and the care and after-care of the sick.

The need for greater independence of local authorities in the spending of money in their own areas has been recognised and provision made for further devolution of responsibility by the counties to the councils of the large districts.

Perhaps the greatest distinction between central and local government is that the Royal prerogative, and the freedom of Parliament, which are so important in the conduct of central government affairs, have no place in local government. A local authority can work only within the powers conferred upon it by the statutes, and if it goes beyond those powers its actions become *ultra vires*.

If, on the other hand, a local authority fails to perform its duties efficiently it becomes subject to the attention of the central government, which can then act by persuasion, by the withholding of financial grants, or, finally, by direct intervention with its powers of default.

Certain central government activities are, by their nature, more closely associated with local government than others. Health and housing are the best examples, but the Minister of Education and Science has the duty of ensuring that local authorities carry out efficiently and effectively the national policy of comprehensive education. Similarly, the Minister of Transport has a direct interest in the construction and the upkeep of roads by the local authorities. These, and other government departments, exercise their powers of supervision and control in various ways. Visits of inspection and local enquiry may be made, and statistics examined. Application for loans and grants may become the subject of special scrutiny. The issue of statutory rules and orders and of circulars, the approval of by-laws, and the auditing of accounts by the district auditors, are among the more formal methods of control.

It is the policy of central government departments to work in friendly co-operation with the local authorities, and the relationship is rather one of partnership than of supervision. It is very rare indeed for the big stick to be taken out of the cupboard and dusted prior to use—but it is there in case of need.

Major Authorities

The various types of local authorities have already been mentioned briefly. The major authorities are the administrative counties and the county boroughs. The minor authorities are the three types of county districts, *i.e.* the municipal or non-county boroughs, the urban districts, and the rural districts, the last named being further subdivided into parishes. Each or these authorities has its local council. The local authorities in Scotland and Northern Ireland are broadly similar, but with somewhat different titles. The arrangement in London is different, for the London Government Act of 1963 established a Greater London Council to replace the administrative counties of London and Middlesex by a Greater London comprising the ancient Corporation of the City of London and new administrative areas known as Greater London Boroughs.

Each local council is composed of the elected councillors with, in some instances, aldermen elected by the councillors. The chairman presides over the formal meetings and has, in addition, various civic duties to perform. In the borough he is, as a rule, the Mayor, and in certain large cities the Lord Mayor. The procedure to be followed at local government elections is set down in the Representation of the People Acts. The qualifications for voting are that the voter shall be over the age of twenty-one, and registered as a local government elector for the area concerned. The register of electors is compiled each year. The procedure for voting is similar to that for elections to Parliament.

Candidates for election to a local council may be independent of any political party or other organisation, and there is still a place for the independent member in local government. Of recent years there has been an increasing tendency towards election on a political party basis, or as the representative of some organisation with local interests, such as a ratepayers' association. Candidates for election must be over twenty-one years of age, of British nationality. The chief disqualifications are the holding of paid office under the council concerned or any of its committees; bankruptcy; imprisonment for an offence for not less than three months, and conviction under enactments relating to corrupt or illegal practices at elections.

It was, until recently, a disqualification for a member of a council to have any financial interest in contracts placed by the authority, but under the Local Government Acts such an interest only debars that member of the council from discussing or voting on any questions relating to those contracts. Any interest of this kind, including the holding of stock or shares in a contracting company, must be disclosed to the clerk of the council, whose duty it is to keep a record of such disclosures.

In order to obtain proper representation on the council, boroughs are usually divided into wards, and counties into electoral divisions, the number of councillors for each ward or division being fixed.

In constitutional law "A local government authority is a body corporate constituted by Act of Parliament and endowed with statutory powers" (Wade and Phillips, *Constitutional Law*). The exception to this rule is a municipal corporation created by Royal Charter. Even so, the charter cannot extend the powers of the authority beyond those conferred by Parliament.

County and county borough councils have a statutory power to make by-laws for "the good rule and government" of their areas, and to prevent and suppress nuisances, but they cannot acquire new powers by these means. These by-laws require to be confirmed by the appropriate ministers before they are brought into use, and it is customary for the central government department concerned to draw up model by-laws for the assistance of the local authorities. By-laws can be challenged in the courts of law and may then be declared invalid, either because they are *ultra vires* or because they represent an unreasonable exercise of power.

Provision of Services

The services provided by the local authorities fall under the headings of environmental, protective, personal, and trading.

Environmental services consist principally of housing, and of health and sanitary services, such as the supervision of water-supplies, sewerage and sewage disposal, refuse collection and disposal, food hygiene, prevention of pollution of the air, the provision of baths and wash-houses, and rodent control. Also under this heading are town and country planning, street lighting, highway construction and maintenance, and public safety on the highways.

Protective services include the fire and police services, and civil defence.

The personal services are essentially the product of the social legislation of the present century. They include maternity and child welfare clinics and nurseries, home nursing, a domiciliary midwifery service, health visiting, home or domestic helps for the sick, the ambulance service, vaccination and immunisation, and the after-care of certain physically or mentally ill persons. Under the welfare services may be mentioned provision for the disabled and the handicapped, and for children deprived of a normal home life. The modern range of educational services would also come under this heading of personal services.

Under the category of trading services may be mentioned passenger transport, the provision of a public water-supply, and certain special services such as harbours and docks.

The responsibilities of the councils of local authorities vary according to their character and size. In general, however, the pattern of internal organisation and administration is the same in all. Matters of policy are decided by the whole council meeting in public session. If it does not wish its deliberations on a particular matter to be made public, the council may resolve itself into a committee of the whole council. Council meetings are held at stated dates and times, and at regular intervals. The proceedings are formal, in accordance with an agenda prepared in advance, and the chief officers are in attendance. Although opportunity is thus given for debate on controversial measures, much of the work of local government is conducted by the committees, so that the various measures before the full council have already been carefully examined, and the reports are usually presented to the council by the chairman or vice-chairman of the appropriate committee. The subsequent debate may tend to take on a political complexion if there are strong party feelings for, or against, the proposals.

The committee system is an essential element of local government, and without it the business of the local authorities could not be carried on in its present form. To replace the men and women who give up their time to serve voluntarily on local government committees, either as elected councillors or as members co-opted for their special knowledge, would require a small army of paid officials. Local authorities may appoint committees for any purpose, general or special, and may delegate to a committee any of their functions, except the power to levy rates or borrow money. With the exception of the finance committee, up to one-third of the members of a committee may be persons who are not members of the local authority.

Committees of local authorities are of various kinds. Statutory committees are those which must be appointed by statute, and they include finance, health, and education. Standing committees are appointed on a permanent basis in accordance with the standing orders of the council and meet at regular intervals. Special, or *ad hoc*, committees may be set up for a limited period or to investigate a particular problem. Joint committees consist of representatives of more than one authority, to deal with problems over a wider area than that of a single council. Committees may be either advisory or executive, their powers and duties being defined in the standing orders of the council.

Local Government Officers

Broadly speaking, local government officers fall into three categories. There are the chief officers, whose duties are mainly administrative and professional, their subordinate officers, and the skilled and unskilled manipulative and manual workers who undertake the technical and physical work of the council.

Each council works to a set establishment of posts, and vacancies are filled within this as they occur. Appointments to senior posts are made by the council, on the recommendation of the appropriate committee, after public advertisement. Junior appointments are usually made, or confirmed, by the appropriate committee on the recommendation of the chief officer concerned. Rates of pay and conditions of service are the subject of national negotiations.

Although local government employees are not subject to the restrictions on their private activities that apply to civil servants, they are expected, as public servants, to maintain a high standard of integrity and especially of honesty. They are legally servants of the council and must, therefore, act under the orders of the council, but there are certain exceptions. The treasurer, for example, must not obey an order to make a payment which he knows is illegal. Similarly, the medical officer of health and the health inspectors have a duty to protect the health of the inhabitants of the area, and they would receive the backing of the Ministry of Health if their employing authority were shown to be failing to support them in this respect.

The clerk to the county council, and the town clerk, are the senior officials whose duty, *inter alia*, is to co-ordinate the work of the other chief officers, and to ensure the smooth running of the administrative machine. In addition, the clerk is usually the legal adviser to the authority. He may also be clerk of the peace, and have other responsibilities in connection with the registration of electors and the process of elections to Parliament. It is, therefore, important that the clerk should have legal training, and these men are usually solicitors with special experience in local government work. The medical officer of health is required to have special experience in the prevention of disease and the promotion of the health of the community. The other chief officers are also suitably qualified and experienced in their professional work, for all will have served in similar, but less important and subordinate, posts after obtaining their professional or academic qualifications.

Unlike the civil servant, the local government officer works for a committee, or committees, which are concerned with day-to-day administration in addition to initiating policy. This system has both advantages and disadvantages. It is true that a relatively speedy decision may be obtained, where needed, by reference to a committee, and the collective experience of its members may be invaluable. On the other hand, a great deal turns on the relationship between the chairman and the chief officer concerned. A strong chairman, with sufficient leisure and interest, may reduce the chief officer and his subordinates to mere shadows. A weak chairman, or one who is too busy with other matters, may result in the chief officer becoming prominent in matters of policy, which are really the concern of the council. The committee system can also become an admirable shield or shelter for officials who do not want to embark on an unpleasant or unpalatable course of action, or to accept personal responsibility.

Finance

As is the case with central government administration, financial considerations play a major part in the affairs of local government

Rates are local taxes paid by the occupiers of land and buildings in a local authority area to help towards paying the cost of local services, and the responsibility for levying and collecting them rests with the county borough and county district councils.

County councils do not collect rates, but levy a contribution from the county districts by issuing a precept for the sum required. Valuations for rating purposes are not undertaken by the local authorities, but by the valuation officers of the central government.

Within the local authority it is the responsibility of the finance committee to exercise financial control. In addition, there is an annual audit of local authority accounts by the district auditors. These central government officers have special responsibilities and powers, for they must disallow any expenditure which is incurred without statutory authority, as well as excessive expenditure within the statutory framework. Any illegal payments must be surcharged personally upon those who have authorised them, *i.e.* the councillors concerned.

It will be seen, from this brief review, that local government has grown from the purely parochial activities of the eighteenth century to a very wide range of public services, which is closely interwoven with the affairs of central government.

CHAPTER XIII

FINANCIAL CONTROL

Public administration, and indeed any type of administration if it is to be efficient, must pay regard to the wise and proper spending of money, and in a modern state the financial control exercised by the central government is a dominant feature in aiding or hindering development. In this chapter it is proposed to consider first the central machinery, before examining the financial control exercised by other bodies, such as the local authorities.

In Britain the Treasury is the key department in this respect, and it dates, in effect, from the office of Treasurer, founded in 1616. In earlier times the King raised money by taxation, with or without the approval of Parliament, and he was then free to spend it as he wished. Even under the Stuart kings the principal struggle by the House of Commons was concerned with the right to control taxation, rather than expenditure, and it was only slowly, during the eighteenth and nineteenth centuries, that the modern system emerged of controlling expenditure through the machinery of estimates, supply, and appropriations in aid.

In constitutional law the whole of the national revenue is the Queen's revenue, but the raising and spending of it is controlled by the House of Commons, a right which is based on the outcome of many long struggles, and which is embodied in the Bill of Rights of 1689 and, finally, the Parliament Act of 1911, which made the Assent of the House of Lords no longer necessary for a bill certified by the Speaker to be a Money Bill. All government revenue is now paid into the government account with the Bank of England, *i.e.* the Exchequer Account or Consolidated Fund, and all payments are made from this fund, with few exceptions. The Exchequer Account at the Bank of England was first introduced by William Pitt in 1787, and the income of the central administration, derived from the proceeds of taxation, of loans, of trading profits, and the hereditary revenues of the Crown, is paid into it.

It is important to remember that the greater part of central government expenditure is authorised from year to year. The exceptions are few and specialised, and they include salaries and pensions of judges and certain senior officials whose independence must be safeguarded. All other expenditure, including that on defence, the social services, and the administration of the country,

116

is subject to the annual vote by the House of Commons to grant "supplies" to the Crown.

Estimates for these supply services, as they are called, are examined by the whole House sitting as a Committee of Supply, with the Chairman of Committees in the chair instead of the Speaker. As the financial year begins on April 5th, this means that each government department must submit its estimates to the Treasury in the preceding November or December, in order that the total estimates may come before the House in February. These estimates are grouped under the headings of "Votes", which are broken down into sub-heads and items. When the House of Commons has approved the estimates, the amounts requested are confirmed in the Appropriation Act, which allocates the money to the specific Votes. Within each Vote the spending of money on a different sub-head from the one mentioned, a procedure known as a *virement*, is allowed, but only with Treasury consent. Distribution of expenditure within sub-heads also requires Treasury approval of the type of expenditure involved. Any excess of expenditure, or a new service not included in a Vote, or a *virement* which the Treasury considers should be brought before Parliament, calls for a Supplementary Estimate, which is examined as carefully by the Treasury and Parliament as the Annual Estimates.

Since the Appropriation Act is not usually passed until some four months after the beginning of the financial year, Parliament authorises a provisional sum to cover interim expenditure by means of a Consolidated Fund Act passed usually about the end of March, and this Act also authorises the Supplementary Estimates for the year just coming to an end.

Payments out of the Consolidated Fund are of three types. There are the recurrent charges already mentioned as being authorised by permanent legislation. These are known collectively as Consolidated Fund Services. The Supply Services are granted annually by the authority of the Appropriation Acts and Consolidated Fund Acts. Finally, there are the Capital Payments, including loans to local authorities and other public bodies. As these moneys are (or should be) recoverable, Parliament gives authority to make loans within a specified total, which may amount to several hundred million pounds.

The machinery for the central control of expenditure consists of the Treasury, the Comptroller and Auditor-General, the Select Committee on Public Accounts, and the Select Committee on Estimates. The right of the Treasury to control expenditure is derived from the responsibility of the Government for its financial policy, and in particular that of the Chancellor of the Exchequer on behalf of the Government. Mention has already been made of the Treasury scrutiny of the estimates. In addition, the Treasury prescribes the general rules to be observed by all government departments for financial and accounting procedure, and it watches closely and continuously all expenditure throughout the year. Similarly, rates of pay and numbers and grading of staffs in, or employed by, government departments are matters of concern to the Treasury.

The Comptroller and Auditor-General is an officer of Parliament, with an independent and permanent post guaranteed by statute. As Comptroller of the Exchequer he, and he alone, can authorise the Bank of England to give credit to the Treasury for payment out of the Consolidated Fund, and he will not do this until he is satisfied that the requirements of the Treasury have received parliamentary approval. As Auditor-General he audits the public accounts, examining each year the departmental accounts to satisfy himself that the public money has been spent for the purpose for which it was voted. His functions have been extended to reporting to the Committee on Public Accounts any instances of waste, extravagance, excess, or irregularity in the accounts of a department.

The Select Committee on Public Accounts of the House of Commons was established by Mr Gladstone in 1861, and it has since acquired wide powers to enquire, in effect, whether full value has been obtained for the money expended, or whether there has been waste and inefficiency. The reports of this Committee may be discussed in the House of Commons, but it is the Treasury that considers and acts upon the recommendations, or returns a reasoned reply to the Committee, explaining why the recommendations cannot be accepted. The Committee can then, if it wishes, make a fresh attack in another report.

The Select Committee on Estimates, also a parliamentary committee, was originally established in 1912, but it has acquired wide terms of reference since that time. Its purpose is to examine the estimates, both as to the form in which they are presented, and also to suggest economies. It acts through sub-committees without an expert staff at its disposal, and it can, of necessity, only be selective in its examinations, so that the estimates for the current year are not affected by it, but rather Treasury control and influence over a period of years.

When money has been released from the Exchequer Account on the authorisation of the Comptroller and Auditor-General, it is transferred to the account of the Paymaster-General, also kept at the

Bank of England, and he authorises payment to the various government departments. Each department draws money from him in one of three ways. The first way is by Payable Orders, in effect, cheques drawn by the department on the Paymaster-General. In the second way, payments at regular intervals are made by the process of "write-off", whereby periodical payments, *e.g.* of salary, are made regularly to the banks of the creditors in accordance with a schedule. The third method is by "Imprest", which is a local account opened on the authority of a departmental finance division, and replenished periodically by payable orders drawn on the Pay Office, and which can be cashed at a local bank. It provides a method whereby scattered offices may retain ready money for cash payments, such as weekly wages.

The Budget

The main sources of income have already been noted. Each year the Chancellor of the Exchequer formally presents to Parliament his proposals for the renewal of, or changes in, taxation. In other words, he "opens" his Budget (originally a bag containing papers or accounts). As the estimates have already been presented to Parliament, the approximate total of government expenditure for the coming year is known, and the Chancellor takes this opportunity to review the general financial position of the country, and to introduce such changes in taxation as he considers desirable on economic grounds to provide a surplus or leave a deficit. To prevent tax evasion, resolutions agreeing to the Chancellor's proposals, with one exception, are passed immediately by the House in its capacity as Committee of Ways and Means, pending their ratification in the annual Finance Act. The exception is the resolution "that it is expedient to alter the law relating to the National Debt". This is adjourned in order to keep the debate open. These resolutions have immediate effect as if embodied in a statute.

The Budget has become, in modern times, a means of controlling, in effect, the corporate life of the nation. By increasing government expenditure without increasing taxation, or alternatively decreasing taxation but keeping expenditure up, the demand for goods and services rises and unemployment tends to be reduced. If expenditure is decreased and the level of taxation maintained, or taxation increased without a rise in expenditure, the demand for goods and services falls and inflation is checked.

Taxes are broadly of two kinds, direct and indirect. Direct taxation, collected by the Board of Inland Revenue, is represented by income tax, surtax, profits tax, and death or estate duties. Indirect taxation, so called because the person who makes, imports, or sells the commodities or services pays the tax and then charges higher retail prices to the consumer, is mainly collected by the Customs and Excise Department. It includes customs duties on imported goods, excise duties on home-produced goods and services, and purchase tax, which affects both home-produced and imported goods. These indirect taxes have come to exercise a double function—the provision of revenue and the protection of goods produced in Britain or in Commonwealth countries. The principal sources of revenue in this connection are tobacco, alcohol, petrol, entertainment, betting, matches, sugar, and the purchase taxes.

A somewhat puzzling reference is made in the Budget statement to "below the line" expenditure. By this is meant capital expenditure, principally in the form of loans to local authorities, the nationalised industries, and the capital expenditure of the Post Office. The receipts are the repayments of these loans, and a deficit forms part of the "above the line" expenditure and is met from ordinary annual revenue or by borrowing by the Government. Any surplus from "below the line" goes to reduce the National Debt. Here also is a powerful means of control, for local authorities may be encouraged to borrow from the government, or, if this is restricted, they are forced to stand on their own feet and borrow in the open market.

The course of events in central government financial matters is, therefore, the preparation of estimates by the departments in October for the Treasury, and the submission of these to the House of Commons in February. Parliament then authorises a provisional sum from the Consolidated Fund to cover interim expenditure, and also for the Supplementary Estimates for the financial year just ending. This is done by means of the Consolidated Fund Act. Four months later, *i.e.* in July, the estimates become embodied in the annual Appropriation Act authorising the sums to be allocated to each department. Meanwhile, Parliament has adopted all the Chancellor's Budget Resolutions except one (see p. 96), but the Budget proposals remain provisional until the Finance Act is passed in July.

Meanwhile, the Appropriation Accounts, with the reports of the Comptroller and Auditor-General on them, are laid before the House of Commons between November and January. The Public Accounts Committee begins to examine them in December and continues until July. Finally, the supplementary estimates are submitted towards the end of the financial year, to be included, as already noted, in the Consolidated Fund Act at the beginning of the new financial year.

This system of central government finance has important repercussions on the local authorities. If, for example, they require to claim government grants for their services, as all local authorities must in fact do unless they are prepared to carry the whole burden on the rates, then the central departments have the right to enquire into the efficiency of the services provided, to inspect them, and to make comments upon them.

These government grants are paid to the county and county borough councils. The services provided for include education, town planning, fire services, child care, road safety, and physical training and recreation. The total sum is allocated each year, but fixed in advance for a period of two or more years. In addition to the general grants there remain separate grants for police and highways, housing subsidies, and rate deficiency grants to aid the poorer local authorities. The power to withhold or reduce grants is a powerful form of central control, but while beneficial in securing some degree of uniformity of services, it could, if too rigid, rob the local authorities of individuality and initiative.

Local Government Audits

A further method of financial control of the local authorities by the central government is by the system of annual audit by district auditors. These officials are civil servants, and their salaries are paid by the State, but they exercise a quasi-judicial function in their duties. They are required to audit the accounts of all local authorities, with the partial exemption of certain boroughs, but even these boroughs must use the services of the district auditors for accounts such as those dealing with education, child care, local health services, motor taxation, rate collection, police, fire, and town and country planning. In effect, therefore the district auditors examine the accounts of all authorities right down to those of parish councils and parish meetings, and also the accounts of the various committees and officers of these authorities.

The statutes governing the audit provide for certain formalities to be observed. The accounts must be made up by the end of each financial year, usually March 31st, although the minister has power to vary the date. The minister may at any time order the district auditor to hold an extraordinary audit, and the authority or person concerned is then given only three days' written notice. For the ordinary annual audit the auditor makes an appointment with the authority concerned to begin on a specified date. The accounts, and all vouchers, are then deposited in a given part of the office of the authority for seven days before the audit begins in order that any interested person, including a professional expert appointed by a ratepayer, may inspect them, and if necessary take copies. Fourteen days' notice of the time and place where the accounts may be seen must be given in the local newspapers, and any local government elector may appear before the district auditor and raise objection to any item in the accounts. The auditor may call, in writing, for the production of all documents which he considers to be necessary.

Any expenditure incurred without statutory authority must be disallowed by the auditor, as well as excessive expenditure on lawful objects. Most important is his duty to surcharge any sum which has not been properly accounted for upon the person liable, and he must also surcharge any loss upon the person whose negligence or misconduct caused it. This includes any loss of interest or charge of interest, *e.g.* by failing to collect rates, through wilful neglect or wilful default. Negligence in this respect has the normal legal meaning of a breach of a duty of care causing loss, and not merely gross negligence.

Illegal payments are surcharged personally upon those who have authorised them, *i.e.* the elected representatives, officers, and servants of the authority. It is not enough to show the auditor the resolution of the council authorising payment and the receipt for this. He must satisfy himself that the resolution itself had legal authority. Thus, there is no general power by which local authorities may make gifts, and in law a retrospective payment to an officer for extra work, without a prior agreement, is made without consideration and is therefore a gift. Naturally, the circumstances vary with each case, but there must be some substantial reason for a departure from normal practice, such as a threatened breakdown of services, or conformity to some national adjustment of salaries and wages.

The auditor strikes an illegal payment out of the accounts, which then fail to balance. In order to restore the balance he surcharges the sum on the individual councillors who voted for the resolution under which payment was made, and they must then refund this out of their own pockets. As noted above, this power of surcharge is limited to the members, officers, and servants of the authority whose accounts are being audited. It cannot be used as a weapon to recover money from any other persons. If expenditure has been sanctioned by the minister it cannot be disallowed and surcharged by the district auditor, but ministerial approval cannot make an illegal payment lawful, and a challenge in the courts could not be met by saying that the minister approved of the payment if there were no legal sanction for it. It does mean, however, that when in doubt an authority may tend to seek the opinion of the central department, and, thus, government control is strengthened here also. Any person aggrieved by the decision of the auditor to surcharge or disallow may require him to state his reasons in writing.

On completion of the audit, the auditor must certify the accounts, and send a report on the audit to the local authority within fourteen days.

An appeal against the findings in the auditor's report may lie either to the Minister of Housing and Local Government or to the High Court, depending on the circumstances, including the amount involved. The auditor's decision may, for example, be wrong in law or in fact. He must confine himself to the legality or otherwise of payments, and he is in no way concerned with policy, however misguided he may feel the council to be. If there is legal authority, for instance, to pay wages to a given class of employee, and the authority decides to pay in excess of the wages prevailing locally, they may be within the law. If, on the other hand, the payments are excessive the expenditure may be deemed to be unlawful, for the council is, in effect, a trustee of the rate-payers' money, and must act in a fiduciary manner. That was the opinion of the House of Lords in the case of the Poplar Metropolitan Borough Council in 1925 (A.C. 578; 33 Digest 20, 83). Clearly, then, the touchstone is whether a legal payment is fair and reasonable, and if the court or the minister is satisfied that the person surcharged acted reasonably, or in the belief that his action was authorised by law, and that he "ought fairly to be excused", he may be relieved wholly or partly from the surcharge. If not so relieved he must pay within fourteen days, and in default the local authority may recover the amount by a distress warrant issued by the justices, followed by the sale of the seized property. A surcharge of over £500 disqualifies the person surcharged from membership of the authority concerned.

Local Government Loans

The third method of control of local government finance arises from the limitations placed on the raising of money by way of loans. The raising of a loan is essential from time to time, for it may be quite impossible to finance new developments out of revenue, or even to maintain existing services in a modern and efficient condition. On the other hand, uncontrolled borrowing would cast an intolerable burden on the ratepayers, who must eventually pay the debt. In general, therefore, local authorities are allowed to borrow in this manner only when the work to be done is of a permanent nature and for the benefit of the people of the area. Statutory control is strict, and the power to borrow may be derived from Parliament by general Acts, or by a private Act applying to a particular authority. The first essential is that the local authority shall clearly have the power to do the work for which it requires money. It may then borrow in order to acquire land, to build, or to undertake other permanent work, provided that the Minister of Housing and Local Government is satisfied that the cost of the work should be spread over a term of years. This general power also extends to any purpose for which a local authority is empowered to borrow money by any Act of Parliament. A county council may also borrow money in order to lend it to a parish council, which thus receives a loan supported by the credit of the county as a whole. In any event, a parish council must obtain the consent of the county council before seeking to raise a loan.

The Minister of Housing and Local Government considers the financial position of the local authority as a whole, and may order a local enquiry to be held into the circumstances requiring loan sanction. This he does for any service, such as education, which would not normally come within his province. When approved, other conditions must be fulfilled. The loan must be repaid within a stated time, and all loans, whether by mortgage, the issue of stock, debentures, or annuity certificates, rank equally as a charge upon the revenues of the authority.

Power is sometimes taken in a private Act to escape the need for sanction by the central department to a loan, provided that the estimates are proved before the Select Committee of Parliament which considers the bill, but even then Parliament will usually insist that returns of the expenditure of the borrowed money must be made to the Minister of Housing and Local Government.

Loans may be raised in various ways, for example, by issuing stock on the Stock Exchange, by internal borrowing, or by private mortgage. Local authorities may also borrow from the Public Works Loan Board, which is financed by the Exchequer and is under strict Treasury control. An indication of the strength of central control may be gained from the fact that the Local Authorities Loans Act, 1945, prohibited borrowing except from the Public Works Loan Board, and only the Treasury could make exceptions to this rule. Later the position was reversed, with authorities, in effect, being forced to borrow in the open market unless they could show why they should not do so. It is interesting to remember that the Public Works Loan Board was first set up in 1817, to aid small authorities which could not borrow on reasonable terms elsewhere. A high proportion of all loans sanctioned by the

Minister of Housing and Local Government are for schools, housing, water, and sewerage.

It will thus be seen that central control over local authority finance is comprehensive, and that the methods of accounting adopted by the local authorities must, to a very considerable extent, be influenced by this. In addition, there are the safeguards of the law to protect trust funds from improper or unauthorised use, and these include the public money received by local authorities, either from rates or from the central government. The Attorney-General may proceed against the authority itself, or against individual members or officers for breach of trust, either to restrain unauthorised expenditure or to recover sums improperly paid. In the latter event he may proceed against the recipient.

There is a statutory duty on all local authorities to keep accounts in an orderly manner, including the nature of the accounts, for example, general and special, and the manner in which payment may be made by the treasurer. County councils are required by law to appoint finance committees, and must prepare an annual budget. These statutory requirements are, in practice, adopted by all local authorities in their standing orders. Internal control of finance is, therefore, maintained by the finance committee, with the treasurer as the chief officer responsible. Borough councils are exempt from the annual scrutiny of the district auditor for some part of their accounts, although they must use his services for accounts relating to education, local health services, and a number of other activities (see p. 121). For their other work they may have their accounts audited by three borough auditors, two of whom are elected annually by the local government electors of the borough, and the third, known as the "Mayor's Auditor", is appointed by the mayor each year from among the members of the council. This system has a number of unsatisfactory features, especially where the auditors are not professionally qualified. Alternatively, they may employ a firm of professional auditors, or they may elect to adopt the system of district audit so that all accounts come under the jurisdiction of the district auditor. In Scotland, all accounts are audited by professional auditors appointed by the Secretary of State for Scotland, and paid for by the local authority.

Lastly, local authorities have been required for many years to make annual returns of income and expenditure to the central government, and it is the responsibility of the Ministry of Housing and Local Government to collect and tabulate these statistics, which are then published. It will be evident that the corruption characteristic of the eighteenth and early nineteenth centuries would have little chance of escaping detection to-day.

The system of central government financial control is dependent on the supply of money from central funds and the consequential right to audit the accounts of the spending of this money. As the money is provided by Parliament on an annual basis, and as the rules for keeping public accounts are prepared in conformity with this, the system of accountancy is not necessarily the ideal for commercial or trading purposes, where the first essential is to combine integrity with a clear indication of profit or loss. The premier requirement of public financial administration is economy, preferably within set rules and precedents. The permanent official, trained to regard himself as a trustee of public money, tends to regard with suspicion any unusual expenditure however laudable it may be, and the trading maxim that it is impossible to make money without spending money has no appeal to him, for it is not his business to make money, but to save it from being wasted. His responsibility is made heavier by the fact that people, in general, are much more ready to spend the money of others than their own, and "public" or "State" funds are peculiarly vulnerable in this respect.

In this chapter we are not concerned with the normal commercial or banking methods applied to private enterprise, except in so far as the state of the nation influences their activities by the budgeting methods already discussed. Purely voluntary organisations, *i.e.* those which receive no help from public funds, are answerable only to their contributors, and to the law governing charitable trusts. Apart from their legal duty to keep proper accounts and to publish these, it is in the interest of a voluntary organisation to do so, for it can then be seen by all to be doing what it was founded to do. Most voluntary societies now employ professional accountants to audit their accounts, a proceeding which ensures that a uniform system is adopted.

Where a voluntary organisation receives only a small donation from public funds there is likely to be no detailed central enquiry into expenditure, but merely a general interest in the efficiency of the administration and in the services provided. When the grant becomes substantial, the interest in expenditure becomes substantial also. When the contribution from public funds becomes the major source of income, the principles of public accounting, already mentioned, come into force, until the situation is reached when the financial arrangements are, in effect, an extension of those normally adopted by the parent government department, with the

Treasury in control. Thus, the staff of the Comptroller and Auditor-General now audit the accounts of many public bodies financed by grants in aid. They also audit the consolidated accounts of the National Health Service. Accounts of local health authorities, however, come under the scrutiny of the district auditor, and the hospital authorities are dealt with by the Ministry of Health Hospital Audit.

Financial Control of Public Corporations

The real problem comes with the newly-created giants, the nationalised industries. Indirect control is, of course, still of great importance, as, for example, the requirement of Treasury consent to the issue of new capital in excess of a stated amount, and of government approval for the import and export of certain goods. The location of industry and the availability of land are also subject to government control, notably through the local planning authorities.

The relationship between the responsible minister and the public corporations established to run the nationalised industries varies. In general, however, the minister appoints the chairman and members of each Board, and lays down general directions as to how the industry should be run. He does not interfere with day-to-day administration, but he requires to be given statistical information and financial accounts as and when he may need them. His final weapon is the issue of a formal directive, and the mere threat of this would normally suffice to make any Board reconsider its actions. Very few such directives have so far been issued.

The minister also expects the corporation to be self-supporting, in that receipts must at least balance the outgoings, and he reserves the right to say, in association with the Treasury, what shall be done with any profits. Long-term loans for capital expenditure are usually advanced from the Exchequer, and advances from the banks are normally restricted to short term requirements. Parliament has the right to debate the annual reports and accounts of these industries, and to probe into their policy by means of parliamentary questions.

Although as a general principle the degree of government control must depend on the proportion of government grant to total income, this is far from being the case in practice. The universities have so far been relatively free from scrutiny, and it may well prove that, in the interests of efficiency, the great industries now under public ownership may also be regarded as enterprises for which the detailed control of central government expenditure is unsuitable.

Among the various controls of private enterprise must be mentioned the Acts dealing with Monopolies, Mergers and Restrictive Practices, which provide for the control of restrictive trading agreements, such as those of common prices, approved lists of dealers, and restriction of production, by the Registrar of Restrictive Trading Agreements, who is an independent officer of the Crown. The Registrar is responsible for bringing agreements before the Restrictive Practices Court for a ruling as to whether or not these agreements are in the public interest. The court consists of High Court judges and lay members. Unless the court can be convinced that the restrictions are reasonable and beneficial they will be declared void, and orders may be made to prevent them from being continued or enforced. The Acts also made it unlawful to maintain resale prices by collective action to withhold supplies, or by other collectively enforced discriminatory arrangements, and strengthened the powers of individual suppliers to enforce their retail prices. Monopolies not within the scope of the Restrictive Practices Court may be referred to the Monopolies Commission for investigation.

CHAPTER XIV

THE CONDUCT OF MEETINGS

There are certain general principles which govern the conduct of meetings, and those attending them, which arise partly from convention or custom, and partly from the rule of law. They apply equally to an emergency gathering together of people in the face of an unexpected crisis, and to the regular routine of meetings of a properly constituted authority.

In the first place, the meeting must be for a lawful purpose, and each person present must observe the ordinary rules of law. In other words, he cannot plead that his actions are excused if the law is broken merely because he did as the others did. If as a result of an assembly of people the peace is broken, or some person is assaulted, the common law, reinforced by statute law, holds good, and the individual is expected to know his responsibilities in this respect.

Thus, in English law an *unlawful assembly* is deemed to take place "Whenever as many as three persons meet together to support each other even against opposition in carrying out a purpose which is likely to involve violence or to produce in the minds of their neighbours any reasonable apprehension of violence" (*Field v. The Receiver for the Metropolitan Police District,* [1907] 2 K.B. 853). This is not so simple a matter as it looks. Men may assemble for an unlawful *purpose,* for example to plan a robbery, without creating an unlawful *assembly.* On the other hand, the meeting may be for a lawful purpose, but if a breach of the peace occurs as a result of holding it then it may well be deemed to be an unlawful assembly, and much depends on the local circumstances.

In the past it was only a step from an unlawful assembly to a *rout,* for under the common law a rout occurs as soon as those taking part in an unlawful assembly take any active step towards carrying out the purpose for which they assembled, and a rout becomes a *riot* at common law when force is used by the people assembled to overcome opposition. In 1715 Parliament introduced the Riot Act, whereby any unlawful assembly of not less than twelve persons which fails to disperse within an hour of the reading of a proclamation by a justice of the peace calling upon them to do so becomes a *riotous assembly.* To take part in a riotous assembly, as defined in the Act, was a felony punishable with penal servitude for life. The Riot Act also provided for an indemnity for any person who, after the hour provided for dispersal had passed, took steps to suppress the assembly. Anyone doing so before the hour had elapsed would be dealing only with a riot at common law (which was a misdemeanour and not a felony), and would be liable in law for the consequences if excessive force were used. These matters are not without significance even to-day.

It goes without saying that a *seditious assembly*, whereby it is sought to incite disaffection, to bring the government into contempt, or to concoct or execute a public conspiracy, is illegal under the common law. There are also various statutes, ranging from the Unlawful Assemblies Act of 1799 to the Public Order Act of 1936, which prohibit such matters as secret societies, unlawful drilling and military training, and meeting in uniforms. An exception was made in the case of freemasonry, whereby meetings were not deemed to be unlawful, provided that the name of the lodge, the place and time of meetings, and the name and description of every member were registered with the Clerk of the Peace each year (sections 5 and 6 of the Act of 1799). Mention may also be made here of the Unlawful Oaths Act of 1798, whereby it became unlawful to take any oath not required or authorised by law.

Attention should also be drawn to section 5 of the 1936 Public Order Act, whereby any person who, in any public place or at any public meeting, uses threatening, abusive, or insulting words or behaviour with intent to provoke a breach of the peace, or whereby a breach of the peace is likely to be occasioned, shall be guilty of an offence. The Act also defined a *Meeting* as one held for the purpose of discussion of matters of public interest or for the purpose of expression of views on such matters, and a *Public Meeting* as including any meeting in a public place and any meeting which the public or any section thereof are permitted to attend, whether on payment or otherwise. The Race Relations Act, 1965, has a similar purpose of maintaining public order. In addition to these general statutes there are measures of local importance, such as the Seditious Meetings Act of 1817 prohibiting the meeting of more than fifty persons for certain purposes within one mile of Westminster Hall while Parliament is sitting, and the by-laws of various local authorities.

Thus meetings may be either *public*, to which the general public, including the press, have access, or *private*, to which people are admitted because they have a right to be there or because they have been specifically invited to attend.

It will be apparent that in English law there is no right of public meeting in a public place, but merely the recognition that

provided the law is not broken by the assembly no one will interfere to stop it. Indeed, under the Public Meeting Act, 1908, and
the Public Order Act, 1936, persons who improperly interfere with
a lawful public meeting commit a criminal offence.

So much for the right of meeting in a public place, but what is
the position with regard to a public meeting in a private place?
To do so without the consent of the owner is, of course, a trespass,
and the remedies for this may take the form of an action for
damages against the trespasser, an order of the Court (an injunction) to prevent the act being done again, or the removal of the
offenders, if necessary by force.

If the owner permits a person to remain on his premises that
person becomes a *licensee*, and the conditions under which the
licence holds good depend on the nature of the contract between
the licensor and the licensee. It follows, therefore, that those who
attend meetings held on private property can do so subject only
to such conditions as the licensor may impose, and the permission
or licence can be withdrawn at any time. If, therefore, a person
attends a meeting on private property he may, unless he has paid
for admission, be asked to withdraw at any moment by those in
charge of the meeting. If he refuses he may be removed as a
trespasser, but any excess of force beyond the minimum necessary
for his removal would constitute an assault upon him.

Where payment has been made for admission it is possible, as
a general rule, to expel only a person who has behaved in such a
manner as to constitute a breach of the conditions on which his
ticket or licence was issued to him, or where the licensor has
reserved the right to revoke the licence arbitrarily. Where a
licence is granted for money, or other valuable consideration, it
holds good only for the person for whom it was intended, unless,
of course, tickets of admission are advertised merely as being for
sale to the general public at large, as in a public concert.

Free Speech

Quite apart from the rights of attending a meeting, there are the
considerations as to what can be said there. Lord Kenyon declared
in 1799 that "the truth of the matter is very simple when stripped
of all ornaments of speech, and a man of plain common sense may
easily understand it. It is neither more nor less than this: that
a man may publish anything which twelve of his countrymen think
is not blamable, but that he ought to be punished if he publishes
that which is blamable. That in plain common sense is the substance of all that has been said on the matter" (*Reg. v. Cuthell*,
[1799] 27 St. Tr. 642). There is, therefore, no *right* of free speech

any more than there is a *right* of public meeting. There is merely the right to say, or write, anything that does not break the law, or interfere with the private rights of another person.

Sedition, blasphemy, and obscenity are criminal offences dating from ancient times. Statutes, such as the Official Secrets Acts, also place limitations in the public interest on what may be said or written.

The average person taking part in a meeting is little likely to be concerned with these major offences, although he may be sorely tempted to "profanely curse and swear" and thus render himself liable to a penalty of one shilling if a day labourer, or five shillings if he is of or above the degree of a gentleman, under the Profane Oaths Act of 1745. More important is the danger that he may utter some statement defamatory of another. Defamation is of two kinds: *libel*, where the record is of permanent character, as in writing or drawing, an effigy, a gramophone record, a wireless broadcast, or a talking film, and *slander* by the spoken word, a gesture, or some unmistakable sound, such as a hiss.

A libel may be both a civil wrong (a *tort*) and a criminal offence. A slander only becomes criminal when it provokes an immediate breach of the peace. Certain types of slander are regarded in law as more serious than others, for example, to allege unchastity in a woman, some filthy disease in a man or woman, unfitness for an office of honour, incompetence in trade or business, or a criminal offence punishable by imprisonment. Generally speaking, however, slander must be injurious to the reputation of the person concerned in the sense of "special damage", *i.e.* measurable in money, and insult, abuse, or acid comment would not, of themselves, be slanderous. Any person speaking in public, however, should beware of innuendoes, for they may recoil unexpectedly. It is not the intention of the speaker that matters, but the fact that defamation has occurred. If a cryptic remark is intended to hit at *A*, but is generally understood to have applied to *B*, it is no excuse to say that is was not intended for *B* if, in fact, *B* has been hurt.

In order to injure anyone a defamatory statement must be published, that is to say, it must be seen or heard by some other person than the one who claims to have been injured. Publication need not be deliberate or malicious, for the statement may equally be made public innocently or negligently, and, of course, anyone who carries the publication further is also liable. Each fresh publication can be the subject of a separate action in law, although there are certain restrictions on the amount of damages that may be awarded in such circumstances.

Anyone rising to his feet to speak critically of another should remember that, if he slanders a person knowing that his remarks will be reported in the public press, he renders himself liable to an action for libel also, for he may be held to have authorised publication, either expressly or by implication.

There are certain well recognised defences to an action for libel or slander. Thus the statement may be justified (*i.e.* justification) because it is true. That alone would dispose of slander provided that it is, in fact, so. If it proved not to be true the injury is likely to be regarded as aggravated and heavier damages awarded. In libel, while justification may dispose of a civil action, it will not suffice to dispose of a criminal charge. It is then necessary to prove both justification and that publication was made in the public interest.

The second defence is that of privilege, a much misunderstood word, for it bears no relation to the statement made but only to the circumstances under which it was made. There are certain circumstances where complete and fearless freedom of speech is essential in the public interest. Under such conditions *absolute privilege* is conferred, with no right of an action even if the statements are false and malicious. Thus protection is given to all those taking part in any judicial proceedings in any court of law, military or civil, and it includes judges, advocates, members of the jury, witnesses, and parties to the action. Similarly, it applies to any Member of Parliament, but only while he is within the security of either the House of Commons or the House of Lords. Parliamentary papers are protected if published with the authority or by order of either House, or in any complete reproduction of such papers by any person. Professional communications between solicitor and client are protected, and so also are contemporaneous newspaper reports of judicial proceedings, provided that they are fair and accurate.

It is also said that communications between officers of State in the course of their official duties are covered by absolute privilege, but it would not, perhaps, be wise for the uninitiated to rely too heavily on this, for the courts might decide to adopt a very strict definition of what constituted an officer of State. People employed by the nationalised industries or in the National Health Service, for example, could not claim the privileges of being civil servants.

Limited protection, or *qualified privilege*, applies in certain circumstances, provided always that there was no underlying malice or improper motive. This decision, as to whether or not qualified privilege exists, can be finally made only by the court after

considering all the evidence in the particular case.   In general, the
protection applies where it can be held that the person making
the statement was under a legal, moral, or social duty to do so.

In the same way it is essential to protect business enterprises,
or some other common purpose, by recognising that communications between the interested parties must be free and frank.   A
common example is the taking up of references before appointing a candidate to a post.   How far does qualified privilege extend
here?   Suppose, for example, that *A* is a mentally unbalanced
person whose misdeeds have involved *B* in serious losses and about
which he feels keenly.   Is *B* justified in telling all he knows and
feels to *C* when the latter takes up *A*'s references?   The answer
is, of course, no.   *B* must be relevant in his reply, he must clearly
be without any prejudice or malice, and he should make reasonably
sure that his comments are only seen by the person for whom they
are intended.   This matter is discussed in more detail elsewhere,
but it may be emphasised here that anyone wishing to give the
name of a referee should first ask that person's permission to do
so.   Having once agreed, the referee should think twice before
calling on his sense of "moral duty" to damn the applicant.

Another common problem is how far a member of some public
body should go in "speaking his mind" about another.   If the
meeting is manifestly concerned with the public interest, or there
is a public duty, then statements made in good faith at the meeting will be protected by qualified privilege.   If, however, as often
happens, the speaker decides to retail his remarks later on to
others not present at the meeting to show what a good fellow he
has been, then he will not be protected.   If a meeting does not
involve the public interest, for example, a meeting of shareholders
in a company, it is particularly necessary to take care if strangers
are present.   The subject bristles with complications, for qualified
privilege holds good only during the actual progress of the meeting.
It ceases the moment the chairman closes it so that comments made
immediately beforehand, or afterwards, are not protected even
though they may be made within a council chamber.

The third defence to an action for defamation is one of fair
comment on a matter of public interest.   The judge must decide,
as a matter of law, whether it is a matter of public concern, while
the jury decides whether the comment is fair.   The word "comment" is important.   It means an expression of opinion and not
a statement of fact.   "If fact and comment be intermingled so
that it is not reasonably clear what portion purports to be inference, he (the reader) will naturally suppose that injurious statements are based on adequate grounds known to the writer, though

not necessarily set out by him" (per Fletcher Moulton, L.J., *Hunt v. Star Newspaper Co, Ltd,* [1908] 2 K.B. 309). In that case it was held that the defence of fair comment could not be successfully pleaded. Facts and comment must, therefore, be kept separate if this defence is to hold good.

On the question of public interest, it must be remembered that anyone who brings himself to the notice of the public cannot complain if he becomes a matter of public notice, however temporary that interest may be. The author, the holder of any public office, or anyone who speaks or lectures in public, must not, therefore, be unduly hurt if he finds his remarks reported in an unfavourable light, or his book criticised adversely, provided that the comment is fair and an honest expression of opinion, and not inspired by malice.

The Press

In this matter of public meetings the representatives of the press have the same rights to attend as any other citizen, but no more. Once admitted, however, they cannot be muzzled, and they are free to make fair and accurate reports on matters of public concern and for the public benefit, subject, of course, to the restrictions on blasphemy and indecency. An aggrieved speaker may request the newspaper concerned to publish a reasonable letter or statement by way of contradiction or explanation. Refusal to do this may weaken the defence in a subsequent action. A further defence is for the newspaper to have published an adequate apology at the earliest opportunity, but this defence cannot be raised unless a sum of money is paid into court at the same time by way of amends.

It is clearly in the public interest to allow the representatives of the press to attend meetings of all bodies concerned with public affairs. The Local Authorities (Admission of the Press to Meetings) Act, 1908, established the right of representatives of the press to be admitted to the meetings of every local authority. "Representatives of the Press" were defined as including duly accredited representatives of news agencies. This Act was replaced by the Public Bodies (Admission to Meetings) Act, 1960, which provided for the admission of representatives of the press and other members of the public to any meeting of a local authority or other body exercising public functions. The bodies to which this Act applies include *inter alia* education committees, regional hospital boards and certain other National Health Service executive bodies, parish meetings, and water boards, in addition to local authorities as defined in the Local Government Acts.

Under the 1960 Act a body may by resolution exclude the public, and thus the press, from a meeting (whether during the whole or part of the proceedings) whenever publicity would be prejudicial to the public interest by reason of the confidential nature of the business to be transacted or for other special reasons stated in the resolution and arising from the nature of that business or of the proceedings.

Apart from these statutory bodies there are occasions when it is not expedient to discuss certain matters openly, and other meetings may be terminated, or halted temporarily, by the council or board deciding to go into committee.   Another device is to divide the agenda into two parts, the formal business and the business in committee.   It is a wise chairman who decides to keep the second half to a minimum, for the press make good friends but powerful enemies, and nothing is resented more quickly than an apparent restriction of their freedom.   The general public, also, does not like secret meetings.

Under very exceptional circumstances one person may constitute a meeting, for example, the single holder of all the shares in a company, or one creditor who has proved his debt may form a meeting of creditors, and one director may constitute a meeting of the board.   It has even been held that a committee meeting may consist of one person.   In general, however, the common law requires a minimum of two persons, and all properly constituted bodies have their own rules, or Standing Orders, to ensure that meetings are properly constituted by the attendance of a prescribed minimum number of persons.   These rules are also necessary to ensure that time is not wasted by lengthy discussion or irrelevant details, and that the proper democratic procedure of a majority vote is adopted.   It follows, also, that proper notice must be given of the intention to hold a meeting to all interested parties, otherwise it would be possible to exclude people likely to be "difficult" by the mere process of failing to notify them.

Standing Orders

Standing Orders, of which a specimen is shown in Appendix I, usually make provision for any possible difficulties which may arise in the orderly conduct of business.   Thus, they may begin by specifying when the ordinary meetings will normally be held, or the date on which the programme for the ensuing year will be drawn up, for example, "the regular ordinary meetings of the Board shall be held on Wednesdays on dates to be fixed according to a programme drawn up in the (—) month of each year".

Provision is then made for the calling of extraordinary meetings, usually by the chairman, "at any time". If he refuses to do so within a given time on the request of a specified minimum number of members, authority can be provided for a given number of members, for instance six or ten, to call a meeting forthwith. As it is essential that someone should preside over and conduct the meeting, it is usual to lay down that the chairman shall preside. If he is not present then the vice-chairman will act, and failing him someone chosen by the members present. In "closed" communities, such as a college or a club, the rules may provide for the senior fellow or member to preside, and so on in order of seniority. The essential is, of course, to have a clearly defined rule to follow. In practice, if one of the purposes of a meeting is to elect a chairman to take the place of one whose tenure of office has expired, the clerk, secretary, or other senior official present, will open the meeting by asking for nominations, with proposer and seconder, and if necessary arrange for a vote to be taken.

Standing Orders usually prescribe for so many clear days' notice to be given of meetings, and of the business to be transacted. Thus, "three clear days at least before a meeting a summons to attend the meeting, specifying the business to be transacted thereat and signed by the Chairman or by the Secretary shall be left or sent by post to the usual place of residence of every member". The precaution may also be taken of ensuring that failure to serve a notice on any member shall not invalidate the meeting, and of seeing that any special or extraordinary meeting does not proceed to discuss any business other than that for which it was specifically called.

The Orders may also prescribe that the names of all persons attending shall be recorded, and that no business shall be transacted at a meeting unless at least one-fourth of the whole number of members is present. A record of attendances is important in order to meet any subsequent challenge that there was not a quorum. It is also necessary where the constitution of the body specifies that anyone failing to attend regularly shall cease to be a member.

Another essential requirement is that a written record of the proceedings shall be made, and that these *minutes* shall be "entered in a book or other permanent record kept for that purpose and, at the next ensuing meeting, shall be submitted for approval as a correct record, and signed by the person presiding thereat". It is for this reason that the first item on the agenda is always the minutes of the last meeting, and until these are approved as a correct record, and signed, it would not be proper to go on to discuss the next item, which is usually "matters arising out of the minutes" or, in other words, any further developments or action taken on the matters discussed at the previous meeting.

Anyone objecting to the accuracy of the written record, for example on the grounds that it contains a mis-statement of what he, in fact, said, must do so before the minutes are signed as a correct record. If, on the other hand, he wishes to ask whether anything has been done in some matter discussed at the previous meeting, he must do so under "matters arising". The universal rag-bag at the end of the agenda called "any other business" cannot properly be used for this purpose.

Motions

Any meeting which does not produce discussion is very dull, apart from the danger that it is merely acting as a "rubber-stamp" to approve the decisions of others. On the other hand, debate can become so acrimonious that tempers become frayed. Again, some member or members may feel strongly, as a matter of conscience, that a certain issue must be forced to a conclusion. The procedure for voting is, therefore, of importance. It is also rather more complicated than one would imagine, especially if there are proposals and counter proposals.

When a course of action has to be decided upon, the members constituting the meeting must first be "moved" to approve it before they can "resolve" to act. It is, therefore, necessary for someone to "move or propose a motion" or, in other words, to express in clear and unmistakable terms what he considers the board or committee should do. Thus, if it is intended to adopt a report which contains recommendations for future action, the appropriate phraseology would be: "I beg to move that the report be approved and the recommendations adopted". It will be noted that a motion implies positive action. A motion to do nothing or "take no action" would be necessary only if, in its absence, the meeting would be committed to doing something which clearly it did not want to do, as, for example, increase its subscription to some fund of which it did not really approve.

To be effective, a motion requires a proposer and seconder. The proposer puts the motion clearly, as noted above, and the person seconding it merely requires to say, in effect, "I second this proposal", and he need not make any further comment unless he wishes. Having received the notice of motion, it becomes the responsibility of the chairman to see that it is fully and properly debated. In order to give the opportunity for this, Standing Orders may contain a clause requiring members desiring to move a motion to send a notice thereof to the secretary at least seven clear days before the meeting, in order that it may be inserted in the agenda for the meeting. It is also customary to make it clear that any motion can be moved, without notice, on any business mentioned on the agenda for the meeting. This is most important, for it would be quite improper for the chairman of a meeting to refuse to accept a motion proposed in the course of the meeting. The motion fails automatically, and does not need to be voted upon, if there is no seconder. If the subsequent debate shows the meeting to be in favour of the motion, or, even more clearly, if there is no discussion, the matter is put to the vote immediately.

Voting

The manner of voting is within the discretion of the chairman. He may choose to accept what is termed oral expression in Standing Orders, but which, in plain English, means "those in favour say, Aye" and "those against say, No", or he may take a show of hands. It is sometimes expedient, and indeed desirable, to take the vote secretly and by paper ballot. Where, for instance, there is the question of election of one of their number to high office, such as president of a society, or head of a college, it would be invidious, and possibly lead to difficulties later on, if members had to record their opinions openly and by name. The practice then is to record the vote on a slip of paper which is unsigned, to fold it so that it cannot be read by others, and to insert it in the ballot-box, or in a container passed round for the purpose. The votes are then counted by scrutineers specially appointed, who are either officers of the meeting or selected members. Alternatively, the chairman of the meeting may call upon the secretary to read out each voting slip aloud so that every member may know precisely how the voting has gone.

By way of contrast to the secret ballot, it may be deemed necessary to impress on members the importance of the matter under consideration, and Standing Orders usually contain provision for members to request that the voting on any question be so recorded as to show how each member present, and voting, cast his vote. It is, in any event, up to any member who feels strongly enough to ask for his vote to be recorded by name.

The question of voting by proxy will be considered later, and it will suffice here to say that Standing Orders may require that "In no circumstances may an absent member vote by proxy". Generally speaking, a simple majority vote is all that is required, that is to say, a majority of those present and voting. Any member may abstain from voting by simply sitting mute, or keeping his hands to his sides, putting in a blank paper, or merely failing to fill in and return a voting paper. It may sometimes be necessary to count the number of abstentions, if only to show subsequently that the support for the motion was lukewarm. Thus, at a meeting attended by some twenty members, six voted in favour of the motion, three against, and the rest abstained from voting. Clearly, there was some reason for this. Either they did not understand the matter under discussion and felt they could not express an opinion on it, or they were not sufficiently interested to take an active part. The record of abstentions may be of value to the parent body, if there has to be further consideration at a higher level.

A simple majority vote conforms to the common law rule laid down in 1693 (*Hascard v. Somony*, [1693] 1 Freem. K.B. 504), but it may be qualified by local regulations, or even by statute. Standing Orders, or the rules of a society, may require a majority vote of all those *present* at the meeting, and under the law relating to bankruptcy strict rules are laid down as to the number of creditors who may agree upon a composition proposed by a debtor, before the court can approve it.

The motion we have been discussing so far is known as the substantive or "original" motion. The chairman can refuse to put it to the vote only if it is too vague, or is capable of a double meaning. It must, therefore, be clear and concise. It should also contain only one proposal, and not be an omnibus. If it contains more than one, these should be clearly distinguished so that, if desired, they can be voted upon separately. By this means the meeting can resolve to act upon (*a*) of the motion, but to reject (*b*) and (*c*). Anyone who does not like the form in which the motion is cast may propose an amendment. This amending motion must be equally precise.

The chairman must decide here, as with the original motion, whether it is within the terms of reference of the meeting; in other words, whether or not the meeting is competent to decide the matter now raised. In principle, he may himself put forward a motion, which then requires no seconder, but, in practice, motions from the chair are put forward on only formal matters, or when the chairman requires confirmation that he has summed up the feeling of the meeting correctly. Here it is necessary to take note of the right of any member to raise a point of order at any time, or, put differently, to ask for the chairman's ruling that the committee or meeting is acting properly and within its powers, and in accordance with its own rules and Standing Orders. A common example is to question whether or not there is a quorum present, or to ask whether the proposed motions come within the original terms of reference under which the committee was set up. The chairman must then act at once. He may consult the clerk or secretary as to the facts, or send for a copy of the rules, and he may allow a brief debate, but the decision is his, for it is final and conclusive. In strict law an amending motion does not require a seconder, but if it fails to find one it is usually dropped forthwith. Another peculiarity of amending motions is that the person who moves an amendment has no right to reply to discussion on it, whereas the mover of the original motion can do so on his motion.

It is possible that a number of amendments may be proposed, in which case they must be voted upon separately and in due order. In certain instances, for example in the voluntary winding up of a registered company, an original motion cannot be amended, but must be accepted or rejected in its original form. In general, however, the chairman must accept an amendment unless he is satisfied that it is *ultra vires*, totally irrelevant, or introduced mischievously or vexatiously. His task becomes difficult when someone moves an amendment to an amendment, for he must first dispose of this, then of the main amendment, and finally of the original motion. He does this by putting each to the meeting for discussion and vote. If the amendment is *approved*, the original motion is modified accordingly, and put to the meeting for final approval. If the amendment is *rejected*, the original motion is brought forward unchanged for further discussion (and, if necessary, for further amendments) before it is finally put to the vote. It will be apparent that by the time several amendments have been discussed many of the members of the meeting may have only a hazy idea of the wording of the original motion. It is for this reason that Parliament adopts a procedure which ensures that the main issue is kept before it by the device of adding, or removing, the words of the amendment to or from the original motion, instead of debating separately-worded amendments. The procedure described above is, however, the customary one.

When a motion or amendment has been proposed and seconded it can be withdrawn by the proposer only with the consent of the meeting, and an original motion cannot be withdrawn while an amendment to it is under debate. No person has a right to speak more than once on the same motion, except the person who "moved" it, and he may reply to the discussion. Once the meeting has made up its mind on the motion, and resolved upon a course of action, it would be troublesome if dissatisfied members tried to upset it. For this reason, Standing Orders usually lay down that notice of a motion to rescind a resolution, or the general substance of a resolution, must be signed by a specified number of members, and if the motion is not accepted by the meeting a time limit may apply, for example, six months, before it is competent for any member to raise the matter again. The parent body may take power, in its rules or Standing Orders, to be able to refer a motion of this kind to a committee of its members.

Formal Motions

Original and amending motions are not the sum total of the methods of debate, and there are various ways of indicating that members have had enough of a particular matter. Thus, any member is free to move "that the meeting do now proceed to the next business" or that "the debate be now adjourned". If a seconder is found to support it the chairman will then put the motion to the vote, provided that he is satisfied that the subject under discussion has been sufficiently ventilated.

A motion to proceed to the next business has certain advantages. It indicates that at least some members of the meeting are becoming restive. If it is rejected, the debate on the main issue can continue. On the other hand, it can be moved at any time, even during the discussion of an amendment, and so prevent a decision from being reached when it becomes evident that the meeting has become hopelessly lost in a fog of its own creating. Standing Orders sometimes provide a time limit, for example, half an hour, before a motion to proceed to the next business can be moved a second time.

A motion to adjourn the debate has the effect of stopping discussion immediately. If it is seconded it becomes the primary question for consideration, and any discussion on the original or any amending motion must give way to it, but it cannot be moved by the proposers or seconders of the original motion and amendments to this. A motion to adjourn the debate cannot be amended, except to alter the duration of suspension, or the time and place of next meeting. As a general rule, matters adjourned are considered at the next meeting, immediately after the minutes.

These methods of cutting short or terminating discussion are known as *formal* motions, because, in effect, they may be formally moved instead of showing some sudden expression of impatience or disgust, or merely getting up and leaving the meeting. More powerful than those already mentioned are the *Previous Question*, the *Closure*, and *Adjournment of the Meeting*.

The curious title of the Previous Question is derived from the effect of the motion "that the question be not now put", for this now becomes previous to the main issue, and it asks whether, in fact, the original motion should be put to the vote at all.

A motion "that the question be not now put" has two rather unusual effects. If it is carried it kills the original proposition so far as that meeting is concerned, and it can only be brought up again at a subsequent meeting as a new proposal. If, on the other hand, the Previous Question is lost the implication is clear, for if members vote against a motion "that the question be *not* now put" then they must agree that it *be* put, and so all discussion comes to an end forthwith.

The Previous Question cannot be moved during discussion of an amendment, but it can be put before any further amendments are moved, and indeed that is its purpose. Any member may move the Previous Question provided that he has not spoken on the original motion. It cannot form the subject of amendment, and it can only be over-ridden by a motion to adjourn the meeting.

The most commonly used formal motion for stopping further debate is called the Closure, by the motion "that the question be now put". If proposed and seconded it is voted upon immediately, although Standing Orders may allow the chairman to call on the proposer of the original motion to reply and "after such reply the original motion and any amendments thereto shall be put forthwith". The motion for Closure can put the chairman in a difficult position, for he must protect the rights of any minority group, which would otherwise be crushed every time it tried to raise an issue for consideration. He must, therefore, be seen to be acting in good faith if he allows this motion to be put.

Parliament has its own peculiar version of the Closure, called the "Guillotine", whereby set periods of time are allocated to the different parts of the subject under discussion, and when the time expires the vote follows automatically. This procedure is sometimes known as "closure by compartments".

A motion that is often made is reference back to the body or committee which prepared the report under discussion. A motion "that the matter be referred back to the committee" is a convenient way of indicating that the meeting is not satisfied with the advice of the committee, or that the information on which the report has been made is incomplete. It is also more courteous than a flat rejection of the recommendation of the committee, and it has the advantage of keeping the subject in existence for further consideration.

Somewhat similar to reference back is the motion that the report under discussion "be laid on the table". This really means that the meeting is not in the mood to discuss the matter, that it does not consider it to be very urgent, or that it cannot make up its mind what to do with it. In the same way, a meeting may decide to "receive" a document when it considers that all it need do is to note its contents.

The most drastic method of action is to move "that the meeting do now adjourn" or, even more effective, "that the chairman leave the chair". In the latter event, the meeting becomes adjourned indefinitely or until the next fixed date of meeting, if these take place at regular intervals. It should be noted that it is a motion to close the meeting, not to get rid of the chairman. If it is desired to do the latter, the motion should be "that A. B. do now take the chair". Lord Hardwicke (in *Stoughton v. Reynolds*, [1736] Fortescue's Rep. 168) laid it down that any meeting had an inherent right at common law to terminate its own proceedings, for, as he said, "the right is in the assembly itself". Nobody can compel a meeting to sit until all its business is finished. If, however, the board chooses to tie its own hands, for example, by its Standing Orders, it is at liberty to do so. Thus, it may introduce some such phrase as "The chairman may, with the consent of the majority . . ." etc., and thereby give him discretion whether or not to accept a motion to adjourn, but, generally speaking, he would be expected even then to bow to the wishes of the meeting.

A motion to adjourn can be moved only by a member who has not already spoken on the issue under discussion, and it cannot be moved by the proposer or seconder of the original motion, or any amendment to it. When it has been proposed and seconded the motion takes priority over all else, including the Previous Question. It may be discussed, but the mover has no right of reply, and no amendment is possible except on the time and place of next meeting.

The chairman's powers to adjourn a meeting arbitrarily are limited even at common law, for cases decided at various times have indicated that his main justification for such a drastic step would be where such violence and tumult had arisen as to make it unsafe for the members to record their votes. Anything less than this might lead to the suggestion that the chairman was actuated by some unworthy motive, such as fear or bias. Lord Justice Chitty laid down in 1894 that "it is not within the scope of the authority of the chairman . . . to stop the meeting at his own will and pleasure" (*National Dwellings Society v. Sykes*, [1894] 3 Ch. 159). Once he has opened the meeting he must go on. If he adjourns the meeting improperly, the meeting itself can then resolve to go on and to appoint a new chairman forthwith. A chairman acting in good faith, and with a due sense of responsibility, can adjourn a meeting if he considers that it is necessary in order to get the business transacted properly, or when it has, in his opinion, completed its business. The courts, however, have always leaned strongly in the direction of calling upon the chairman to answer for his conduct if he behaves arbitrarily. "Strong" chairmen should remember the old common law rule quoted above that the right to direct the adjournment must be in "the persons which constitute the assembly".

CHAPTER XV

THE CONDUCT OF MEETINGS (*continued*)

The Quorum

In addition to the formal motions by which the conduct of business may be regulated, it is open to any member to question whether a meeting is properly constituted. Thus, he may rightly enquire whether there is a quorum. At common law at least two people must be present to constitute a meeting, but Standing Orders usually specify more than this number in some such form as "Except when approved by the Board business shall not be transacted at any meeting of any Committee or Sub-committee of the Board unless at least one-fourth of the Committee or Sub-committee is present. Provided that in no case shall the quorum of the Committee or Sub-committee be less than two persons". Even this provision may not comply strictly with the common law provision that the acts of a corporation must be done by the corporators, corporately assembled. Unless, therefore, there are specific rules or Standing Orders, it may be requisite that there should be a majority of members present if the meeting is to be properly constituted. It is for this reason that any constitution or articles of association are careful to specify what constitutes a quorum, and where the matter is of legal importance, as in bankruptcy, Parliament may specifically refer to the subject in the appropriate statutes.

The quorum must be composed of members who have a right to take part in that particular business. It would be useless, for example, to introduce a member of the Building Committee to provide a quorum for the Finance Committee if, in fact, he was not a member of the latter, even though he was a member of the parent body to both committees, unless, as is most unlikely, there is some clause in the rules to allow of this.

In the absence of a quorum the meeting is invalid, and the business transacted cannot be recognised either within the affairs of the body concerned or outside of it. In that event, a third person may not be able to take legal action against the board, authority, or corporation, in its corporate capacity, for any action authorised by the ineffective meeting. Much depends on the individual circumstances, however, and, particularly, whether the third person had acted in good faith and with no knowledge of the irregularity.

In general, it is customary to wait for a while to see if more members arrive before declaring that the meeting cannot be held in the absence of a quorum, although this is not essential, and any member insisting on the appropriate number at the exact moment for which the meeting was announced would be within his rights, and the meeting could not then be held. There is no question of adjournment in such circumstances. It must be called afresh, unless the written constitution specifically refers to the meeting as "standing adjourned" in the absence of a quorum being present within a specified period of time. Depending on the circumstances it is sometimes possible for a meeting with insufficient numbers to form a quorum to continue to transact the business, leaving it to the chairman and full committee or parent body to "whitewash" their actions by adopting their recommendations. Such a procedure has its value in saving the time of officials and the members present but it must be the exception and not the rule.

It is not an uncommon experience for members to leave a meeting, one by one, before the business has been completed, particularly if many of them have come from a considerable distance. In such an event, any member may raise a point of order as to a quorum, and the chairman must then order a count. It may be held that the quorum present at the beginning of the meeting was sufficient, but the rules may specify that in the absence of a quorum business must stop, and the meeting is then adjourned. It is interesting to note that in Parliament business is effective in the absence of a quorum, and the Speaker does not notice the absence of members until the matter is brought formally to his attention and the House is then "counted out".

Once a meeting has been adjourned it can complete only the business of the original meeting, and it is then an integral part of it so that any faults in that meeting apply equally to the adjournment. In other words, it could not be pleaded that they were separate and distinct meetings. Terminology is important here, as elsewhere. An *adjourned* meeting is one that has begun, and a *postponed* meeting one that has not. When begun, business must go on, and any administrator using these terms loosely might well find himself in difficulties if he "postponed" a meeting already adjourned to a given day, for it has been known for members to assemble in spite of the notice, and to pass resolutions subsequently held to be valid in law. From this it appears that once a meeting has been convened it cannot be postponed, but should be held and adjourned.

Naturally, these strict rules are held to apply particularly to important public or official meetings. No one is likely to object to the use of loose terminology by the secretary of a local tennis club, for example, but even here it is as well to be precise, particularly if financial matters are to be discussed. It is where there is a specific duty, or where there are specific rights, that any arbitrary action is out of place. To write "cancelled" across a notice of meeting of an athletic club on the screen in the junior commonroom is very different from arbitrary action of a similar nature on the part of a public corporation. A glossary is not out of place here. Once begun a meeting cannot be postponed, it can only be adjourned, and even adjournment *sine die* is still only an adjournment. A meeting ends when its business is finished. It is then *dissolved*.

Notice of Meeting

It follows, from what has been said above, that any notice calling a meeting must obey certain rules. Thus, it must be clear and precise as to the time and place of the proposed meeting, and the kind of meeting that is to be held. It need not specify the order of business in detail, for that is the function of the agenda. Notice must be given in due, *i.e* reasonable, time, and what is reasonable is governed by the circumstances or, more important, by the written constitution of the body concerned. For example, if Standing Orders require a written summons to attend to be sent at least three clear days before the meeting, it would be quite improper for the chairman to call the members together by telephone at a few hours' notice, unless the circumstances were very extraordinary indeed, and in that event he would, no doubt, take steps to have his action ratified at the next formal meeting.

The more responsible the meeting the more necessary it is to observe the formalities. Where there is any legal duty to meet, failure to give proper notice could invalidate the meeting. In the words of Lord Coleridge: "The notice is served not for the personal benefit of the recipient, but as an admonition to him to perform public duty, and a person undertaking a public office cannot exempt himself from those admonitions" (*Rex v. Langhorn*, [1836] 4 A. & E. 538). A member cannot say, in effect, "I do not wish to have notices of meeting served upon me", for he may one day find that his action in so doing has invalidated the proceedings if there is any public duty involved. His proper course would be to resign, or to seek leave of absence from the affairs of the body for a given period of time. The only exception to proper service of notice that the courts would be likely to recognise is one where it was manifestly impossible to secure service of it.

If all members attend without having received a proper summons to do so, and they then agree to proceed with the meeting, a valid meeting can be held. In other words, if the notice specifies a meeting at 3 p.m. on June 14th, and the members all agree to meet at 4 p.m. on July 15th, and they duly attend and signify their consent, a proper meeting can be held. A casual meeting, called on the spur of the moment on the lines, "well, we are all here, what about settling the matter now?", will not do. Such an informal meeting would require to be approved at a subsequent formal meeting, even if it fell within the terms of the constitution of the body concerned.

Standing Orders sometimes specify that "want of service of the notice or summons on any member shall not affect the validity of any meeting". Even so, the notice itself must be sent, it must be clear and precise, and it must not be conditional. To say that a meeting will be held "if certain circumstances arise" would be taken to be inadequate notice. In the interpretation of a notice the words "clear days" mean what they say. In the example given above, three clear days means three days *after* the day of service, *i.e.* after the day of receipt, and *before* the day of meeting. Anyone feeling himself aggrieved at failure to receive proper notice should protest at once, for if he delays until the last moment he may cause much inconvenience by delaying the meeting or causing it to be held invalid, and he would be likely to lose the sympathy of everyone, including the courts.

A notice convening a meeting has been held to be valid, as to the business to be transacted, for an adjournment of that meeting. In other words, notice of an adjourned meeting need not specify the nature of the business, if this was clearly stated on the original notice, but in that event no new business can be undertaken, for the nature of this must be clearly set out in the notice. If an adjourned meeting does proceed to business not specified in the notice, it is only the latter which is invalid, and not the whole meeting.

Voting by Proxy

Allied to the question of notice of meeting is the right to nominate a substitute or *proxy* to attend and vote on behalf of an absent member. The common law does not recognise this right, and it is not customary in public or local government work. It is, however, recognised in company law, which gives a statutory right to a member of a company having a share capital to appoint a proxy. The proxy need not be a member of the company. Subject to the statutes, companies in their Articles of Association usually take power to allow their members to vote by proxy, and proxies may be "general", with a general power to vote, or "special", when the power is limited to a particular item of business. The kind of proxy may also be specified, for example, it may be limited to another member of the organisation or body concerned.

Naturally, only one vote can be cast, even if both the proxy and the original member attend the meeting. In general, the proxy must then give way. A proxy cannot put up both hands—one for himself and one for his friend—in a show of hands, even if he has himself the right to vote. In other words, he can only give one vote on a show of hands, but if votes are recorded by poll he can record his own also. Any regulations allowing proxies almost invariably require the appointment to be made in writing, by a proxy paper. Voting by proxy at parliamentary and local government elections is controlled by statute.

A proxy may help to form a quorum provided that he is counted only once, but he may not count as two persons although also present as a member in his own right. Even here, however, power may be taken specifically to exclude proxies from forming part of the quorum.

Agenda

Having dealt with the rights of members to hold, speak at, and attend meetings, it is necessary to consider next how the meeting is to be conducted. The first essential is an orderly arrangement of the business, preferably made known in advance, so that those attending the meeting may see precisely what they have to consider. This is done by means of an agenda, which, unlike the notice convening the meeting, has no legal importance, but is merely an essential requirement for any well-conducted meeting. The agenda cannot be used as an instrument for widening the scope of the meeting. Even the miscellaneous item "Any other business" at the end of the agenda must conform to this rule.

Reference to the agenda will appear only incidentally in any written constitution, for, as stated, it is not of legal interest, but custom has crystallised the form taken. Thus, the various items will run roughly as follows:—

1. *Appointment of Chairman*, unless already done at some earlier meeting. If not already appointed, it will be open to a member to propose that "A. B. take the chair", and if seconded and approved by a majority vote, A. B. then becomes chairman for the meeting. Where the appointment is for a period of time,

rather than for one meeting, the secretary or other principal officer present may say at the time specified for the meeting to begin, "Ladies and Gentlemen, it is time. May I have nominations for the Chairmanship"; and the procedure already noted is then followed. Experienced members have been known to arrive late on such occasions, for it is difficult to nominate an absentee unless, of course, he has been consulted beforehand and his wishes ascertained—a wise and kindly procedure, for the office of chairman is not one sought by all, as will appear later.

2. *Appointment of Vice-Chairman.* This may be the first business of the new chairman, and he may invite nominations, or if he feels confident enough move a nomination from the chair. In the latter event he needs no seconder.

3. *Notice of meeting and apologies for absence.* The chairman should now outline the purpose of the meeting, either himself, or by asking the clerk or the secretary to read the notice convening the meeting. This is necessary so that there shall be no misunderstandings. Next he takes apologies for absence and, where the constitution requires this, the reasons for their absence. Thus, some bodies may require "good and sufficient reasons" to be approved by the meeting, instead of a mere apology for absence. Such a provision is usually linked with one to the effect that absence on more than a specified number of occasions disqualifies from further membership; a procedure not without its value, for everybody likes to feel that he can resign, but nobody likes to be thrown off.

4. *Minutes of the Last Meeting.* The chairman now calls upon the clerk or the secretary to read the minutes of the last meeting, if any, and asks the formal question, "Is it your pleasure that I should sign these minutes as a correct record?". Anyone who objects, for example, on the ground that a decision recorded there is not correct, or because his name is not stated as being present at the last meeting, should do so now. In the absence of any objection, the chairman signs the minutes and puts the date with his signature.

5. *Matters arising from the Minutes.* These may include the resumption of any adjourned business or the consideration of any fresh circumstances arising since the last meeting. For example, a member may have promised to make some special enquiries on a matter then under discussion and he will, at this stage, report on his enquiries.

6. *et. seq. Current Business.* The meeting now turns to its present business, item by item. It is here that the art of chairmanship may manifest itself, for the good chairman will have gone through all these items with the officers concerned before the meeting. He may even have taken the trouble to revise the order of business so that the meeting may settle comfortably, and not be thrust at once into an uproar over a contentious matter. There are usually one or two main items and a number of minor ones, and it is best to put the really important matters in the middle of the agenda. If they come at the beginning, they may cause heat to be generated early on, or they may not receive adequate discussion because members are still feeling shy and strange to the meeting. If taken at the end, when members are getting tired, the main issues may become obscured by minor and irrelevant points of detail.

Some people seem to have a kind of inward compulsion to speak on all possible occasions, whereas others sit mute and can be induced to comment only by tactful persuasion by the chairman. As it is the latter who are usually the more know-ledgeable, and sometimes the most vocal after the meeting, it is part of the duty of the chairman so to manage the discussion that the tiresome ones do not monopolise it and the silent ones are encouraged to comment. Above all, he must know when the time has come to close the discussion and take a vote. There is a moment in all discussions when everything constructive has been said, and members begin to repeat themselves.

Any Other Business. This is the final item on the agenda, and it enables members to introduce matters within the terms of reference of the meeting, or in accordance with the notice convening it. If skilfully phrased, almost anything can be introduced here, and the chairman must be wide awake if he is to prevent any item under discussion from being *ultra vires*.

The procedure described above applies equally to committees and sub-committees. Each must have its chairman and its agenda if it is to do its work properly. Although Standing Orders usually prescribe that the chairman and vice-chairman of the parent body shall be *ex-officio* members of every committee appointed by it, they do not normally take the chair at such meetings. There are many advantages in appointing separate chairmen for committees, for the load on the principal chairman would otherwise be intolerably heavy, and he can gather round him a select body of experienced people, any one of whom can deputise for him on some particular aspect of the work. A specimen agenda is shown in Appendix II.

Duty of a Chairman

The duty of a chairman has been judicially defined. "It is the duty of the chairman, and his function, to preserve order, and to take care that the proceedings are conducted in a proper manner, and that the sense of the meeting is properly ascertained with regard to any question which is properly before the meeting" (*National Dwellings Society v. Sykes*, [1894] 3 Ch. 159, per Chitty, J.). The recurrence of the word "proper" in his Lordship's mind is interesting, in that the chairman must, by inference, see that nothing is done improperly. What, then, are his powers? He may order the removal of anyone who disturbs the proceedings or threatens to do so. If the chairman authorises force, and this is excessive, he will be liable to damages for assault. In the event of a breach of the peace the offender may be charged with this, and given into custody. There must, however, be a breach, or a reasonable apprehension of this, otherwise an action for false imprisonment may follow.

If a member, who is rightfully present, deliberately obstructs the business of the meeting, the chairman can accept a motion, and the meeting can resolve, to suspend or exclude him, if necessary by force. There is little doubt that a chairman who expelled a member on his own authority would be within his powers if the circumstances warranted it. In the last resort he can adjourn the meeting.

In addition to these legal powers there are certain conventions which strengthen the authority of a chairman. All remarks are addressed to him, and questions are asked through him, usually by the formula: "I should like to ask Mr C. D., through you, Mr Chairman, if . . .". For the duration of the meeting his decision is final on any point of procedure, and in the event of a tie in the voting he usually has an additional vote, known as a casting vote. Finally, the chairman acting honestly and in good faith is not liable if he makes a mistake in the conduct of the meeting.

The question of a casting vote merits more detailed consideration. The common law principle is one person one vote, and, as mentioned earlier, this may be given by a show of hands in answer to the request by the chairman that "all in favour signify by raising the right hand", and, similarly, for those against the motion. Alternatively, there may be a reply by voice, as in some university and parliamentary proceedings. Thus, in one ancient university, anyone disapproving of a measure may rise at the appropriate moment and say *non-placet*, and this is the signal for those supporting the motion, *i.e.* those voting *placet*, to move to one side of the Senate House and those voting *non-placet* to move to the other. The issue is then decided by counting numbers, or, if the press of people is too great, by resorting to a card vote. Similarly, in Parliament, the volume of those calling "Aye" or "No" may decide the issue, or it may lead to an actual division, when the members present and voting go through one of two lobbies, marked either *Ayes* or *Noes*, and are counted as they leave by the "tellers" appointed for the purpose.

It is common practice for a chairman of any meeting to accept a chorus of "Ayes" as signifying approval, but to resort to a show of hands or to a ballot if those against are numerous, or press for a more careful scrutiny by means of a poll. There is a common law right for any voter to demand a poll (literally a counting of "polls" or heads), and this right is sometimes incorporated in statute law, as in the Companies Acts, when a poll may be demanded by anyone present and competent to do so, as a challenge to the chairman's ruling that a motion has been carried or lost. In the event of a written vote, the validity of any given vote must turn on the circumstances, but in general the ruling of the presiding officer, or chairman, will be conclusive on this. In an election of named persons, for example, a mistake in completing the return correctly will invalidate it, unless permission is immediately asked to correct it, and the chairman agrees. A mistake brought to light *after* the election results have been declared cannot be considered, unless it is due to a fault in the procedure or in the wording of the voting paper, in which case the whole election may be invalid. Any departure from a simple straight vote of *yes* or *no*, or for M or N, should be clearly agreed upon before voting begins. Thus it may be convenient, in exceptional circumstances, to take an informal "straw" vote, in which blank voting papers will also be counted, as a clear indication of the number of abstainers and as an indication of the feeling of the meeting. Where this is done the presiding officer must make quite clear what is intended.

It sometimes happens, also, that after a long discussion, with many motions and counter-motions, the members of the meeting may be uncertain as to precisely what they are voting upon. It is for the chairman to tell them, and preferably to read out the resolution as drafted by the secretary. If he does not, then any member in doubt has the right, and indeed the duty, to demand the precise wording of the motion, or the purpose of the vote.

Once a poll has been demanded it should go on, even if all candidates but one withdraw, for it has been held that an election on a show of hands was not valid if a poll had been called for subsequently and not taken, even though only one candidate remained and had already been approved by a majority on a show of hands. Similarly, refusal to take a poll vote when demanded may invalidate the election or resolution.

There are certain clear advantages in demanding a poll, particularly to a candidate, or the mover of a resolution, who has lost by only a small margin on a show of hands. In a poll it may be possible to enlarge the numbers of voters by including all the members absent from the original meeting. This is quite legitimate, for the poll is simply an expansion of the earlier meeting, so that all those *entitled* to attend it may take part in the poll. Similarly, proxies can cast their own and their proxy vote in a poll, but not on a show of hands. It should be noted that a poll is intended to make the results of the voting clear beyond all doubt. A secret ballot, in which the identity of the voter is hidden, is not, therefore a poll under the common law and the taking of a poll by secret ballot in local government and parliamentary elections is governed by statutes.

As the common law principle is "one person, one vote", it follows that a chairman can only have a casting vote if it is specifically given to him by the regulations governing the meeting, for a casting vote is a second vote. If he abstains on the first occasion, and then casts his vote to settle a tie in the voting, that is his original vote and not a casting vote.

Although the chairman may be endowed with a casting vote, and nearly all chairmen of statutory bodies are so endowed, he need not use it. Indeed, the wise chairman will use it to settle an issue only if it is in the interests of the meeting as a whole that he should do so. Where there is no strong consensus of opinion, or where the opinion of the meeting is sharply and apparently irrevocably divided so evenly that only a casting vote can decide the issue, then the best course is often to let well alone. A chairman can use his casting vote any way he wishes, even against his earlier original vote.

It goes without saying that a chairman elected by the meeting can be removed by the meeting, and such a power would undoubtedly be supported by the courts as being essential to the "good order and management" of a meeting if the chairman proved to be incompetent, partial in his dealings, or maliciously obstructive. This common law right may be incorporated in the written constitution of the body concerned.

An individual member, however, cannot demand recompense for damages sustained as a result of the action of a chairman, for the courts will assume that the majority of those present at the meeting will have the good sense to ensure that the chairman behaves according to their wishes. The courts will therefore correct the conduct of the meeting as a whole, for example by way of injunction to prevent its decision taking effect, if the procedure has been irregular, but they will not step in to reverse a decision harmful to one individual or a minority of members. Even where the procedure has been wrong the courts will respect the wishes of the majority, provided there has been no underhand action. Of course, if a chairman is so foolish as to interfere with the obvious rights of a member, for example by refusing to allow him to propose an amendment or to cast his vote, he must not be surprised if the courts intervene on the ground that in this instance the majority could not be expected to put the matter right.

Minutes

Finally, it is necessary to consider the recording of the proceedings of the meeting. These are known as the Minutes. There is no common law insistence on a permanent record, but the disadvantages of not having one are so obvious that power is almost invariably given, even sometimes by statute, to ensure that this is done. It is so easy for people to forget, or gloss over, what they have said. At least one dignified body now asks speakers to send in a précis of their remarks, in addition to recording them verbatim by means of a shorthand writer and a recording machine. This apparent excess of caution proved to be necessary after a speaker denied the accuracy of the shorthand report.

Terminology must be respected here, for there may be a difference between the minutes of a meeting and a report of the meeting. Minutes need only record the name, date, time, and place of the meeting and the matters agreed upon, whereas a report can include every word uttered. Unlike a report, which can be short or long and may give merely the broad trend of a meeting, the minutes must be precise, and Standing Orders may contain an item as follows: "The minutes of the proceedings of a meeting shall be drawn up and entered in a book or other permanent record kept for that purpose, and, at the next ensuing meeting, shall be submitted for approval as a correct record, and signed by the person presiding thereat". Specimen minutes may be found in Appendix III. It will be seen that the essentials are to record the exact nature of the meeting (*e.g.* the 49th Meeting of the —— Board), the time and place, the name of the chairman and of others present, the matters decided ("*Resolved*", etc.), time of conclusion ("there being no other business the meeting closed at ——"), and date of next meeting, if any.

There is no legal requirement to confirm the minutes of the previous meeting, and failure to do so does not invalidate the decisions taken at that meeting. A request by the chairman for authority to sign the minutes as a correct record cannot be used as an excuse to challenge the proceedings and findings of the previous meeting, whereas a report similarly submitted for approval could be so used.

Minutes kept in proper form, and duly signed, will be recognised in law as evidence of the proceedings, but they could, of course, be challenged in the courts if it could be shown that they were not, in fact, a correct record, just as, for example, a resolution can be proved to be valid although it was omitted from the minutes. The constitution sometimes lays down that the minutes shall be conclusive evidence without further proof, but even this will not protect them from challenge by someone who was not a party to the proceedings so recorded.

It cannot be over-emphasised that the minutes are merely a correct record. They cannot be produced to show conclusively that the meeting was conducted properly, and they certainly would not make a faulty notice of intention to call the meeting into a valid one.

Common sense demands that minutes should be written up within a few hours of the meeting, while the subject is fresh in the secretary's mind. Human nature being what it is, some men keep rough notes and then draw vividly upon their imagination a few hours before the notice of the next meeting is sent out. It should be noted that the courts will not approve of such human frailty. Minutes must be written within a reasonable time of the meeting to which they relate, otherwise they become merely a feat of memory. It is a wise and sensible practice to circulate the draft of the minutes to members present, or entitled to be present, as soon as possible after the meeting. By this means the secretary can be made aware of mistakes and correct these when the chairman uses the formula, "the minutes of the last meeting have been circulated, is it your wish . . .", etc. It also has the useful effect of telling those present what they did in fact decide upon—a very necessary procedure, particularly for those who have acquired the art of sleeping at meetings.

The procedure outlined in this and the preceding chapter applies equally to committees, but it is usual to require, in Standing Orders, that proceedings in committee shall be confidential by requiring, for example, that "A member of a Committee shall not disclose a matter dealt with by, or brought before, the Committee without its permission until the Committee shall have reported to the Board or shall otherwise have concluded action on the matter", and not even then if the parent body resolves that the subject is to be regarded as confidential. If members cannot be trusted to observe this rule much harm can be done, particularly when such matters as the appointment of officers, or the making of contracts, are concerned.

Disclosure of Interest

Members of public bodies in particular must constantly be on guard against any appearance of soliciting or recommending persons for appointment by any other than the accepted method of a written testimonial or reference as to the ability, experience, or character of the candidate. Relatives of members and officers seeking appointment are expected to disclose, preferably in writing, the fact that they are so related. Members must similarly disclose a relationship to any candidate, for this becomes an "interest" (*vide infra*). Standing Orders may go so far as to specify that "Two persons shall be deemed to be related if they are husband and wife or if either of the two or the spouse of either of them is the son or daughter or grandson or grand-daughter or brother or sister or nephew or niece of the other, or of the spouse of the other". Nowadays, canvassing of members of any board or committee for any appointment usually disqualifies the candidate automatically.

A pitfall for the inexperienced is when to disclose an "interest" in the business under discussion. It is a most important matter, which has to be decided at once, for the courts may take a stern and rigid attitude towards anyone failing to disclose an "interest", particularly in financial matters, and they may decide that an apparently remote interest is relevant. For this reason, Standing Orders are usually precise. The appropriate section may be headed "Interest of Members in Contracts and Other Matters" (note the words "other matters").

"If any member of the Board has any pecuniary interest, direct or indirect, in any contract or proposed contract or other matter and is present at a meeting of the Board at which the contract or other matter is the subject of consideration, he shall at the meeting, as soon as practicable after the commencement thereof, disclose the fact, and shall not take part in the consideration or discussion of, or vote on any question with respect to, the contract or proposed contract or other matter and shall retire from such meeting unless the Board invite him to remain. If any question should arise as to what in any circumstances amounts to a direct or indirect pecuniary interest, the Chairman shall adjudicate on the issue and his decision shall be final." The officers are similarly expected to declare any pecuniary interest, direct or indirect. "In the case of married persons living together, the interest of one spouse shall, if known to the other, be deemed to be also the interest of that spouse."

Although these provisions are mainly concerned to prevent nepotism and fraud, and to ensure that members behave with transparent honesty and integrity, the principle of declaring an "interest" can be safely carried even further. It is common experience, particularly in smaller towns and cities, for the same people to sit on a number of different public bodies. From time to time the interests of these bodies may conflict, for example in competition for land or buildings or for the services of some particular officer. Although there may be no legal requirements to do so, members may have a moral obligation to disclose that they are "interested" in some other capacity in the matter under discussion.

Estimates and Tenders

A highly technical matter, and one which confuses many people, is the procedure with relation to estimates, tenders, and contracts. The first essential is to ensure that everyone has "clean hands", as the old rule of law in equity would put it. Next, the legal requirements must be strictly observed, and, finally, any action taken must be in conformity with the constitution as embodied in the Articles of Association or Standing Orders. These are usually quite precise, *vide* Specimen Standing Orders, Appendix I.

It is usual to direct that written estimates of the probable cost of any work contemplated shall be provided by the officers, and that these should include the initial or capital expense as well as the current or subsequent running costs. The officers may prepare these estimates themselves or obtain them from experts, such as architects or engineers, employed for the purpose. When the authority concerned has made up its mind what it wants, and whether it can afford it, the matter is put out to tender. In other words, contractors are invited to bid for the work. Tenders may be invited by advertisement in the public press so that anyone may apply. Alternatively, the authority may maintain an approved list of contractors, for example for building and engineering works, which includes all firms who have applied for permission to tender, and who have satisfied the authority that they have the necessary capacity and conditions of labour. This approved list is usually reviewed each year after notice has been given by advertisement in the public press. Where an approved list is kept, all contractors on it are asked if they wish to tender for the work concerned.

The authority may take power to restrict the list, for special reasons, to firms known to be suitable for the particular type of work involved, but in general it would be expected that the larger the contract sum the bigger the list of firms invited to tender, and for large amounts, for example £100,000 and upwards, it would be natural to invite tenders from ten or twelve different firms, or to advertise for tenders in the national as well as the local press.

It is usually provided that tenders shall be submitted in plain sealed envelopes, with no marking to indicate the sender, but franked with the word "Tender" and the subject to which it relates. The secretary or clerk to the board then keeps these envelopes in safe custody until the time appointed for their opening. At the appointed time the tenders are opened in the presence of approved persons, commonly the senior officials, including the treasurer, who then initial the tenders and prepare a list, similarly initialled, for the information of the members of the authority, board, or committee.

The general rule is that the lowest tender must be accepted (or the highest if the authority is receiving the payment). Any departure from this rule must be for good and sufficient reason, and the decision should be recorded in the minutes. "Good and sufficient" reason may include the view, honestly held, and arrived at in good faith, that the contractor submitting the lowest tender has been over-optimistic in the time allowed, or has clearly miscalculated the magnitude of the project. Again, use may be made of local knowledge that he is in difficulties in fulfilling his existing obligations, either for financial reasons or because of an inadequate labour force. Whatever the reasons, a public authority must be ready to demonstrate beyond dispute that it has acted in the public interest in rejecting the lowest tender in favour of a higher one.

When the tender has been accepted, a formal document, or contract, is prepared which specifies the work to be done, the materials to be used, the price to be paid, and the time when the work is to be completed. In addition, there may be clauses to allow damages to be paid to the contractor if the authority breaks the terms of the contract, or for security to be required of the contractor for the due performance of the contract. Where provision for damages or security is to be required the form of tender should indicate this quite clearly, so that the contractor knows precisely where he stands when preparing his tender. Provision may also be made to ensure that the contractor does not assign or underlet the contract without the written consent of the authority, and also that goods and materials used shall conform to approved standards.

Clauses may be inserted giving the authority power to cancel the contract, and recover any loss, if the contractor gives any gifts or inducements in relation to it, or if he fails to deliver goods or materials within the time specified. It is customary, also, to insert a "fair wages" clause. This ensures that the contractor pays rates of wages, and observes hours and conditions of labour, not less favourable than those established for the trade or industry in the district, and that he shall recognise the freedom of his workpeople to be members of trade unions. If at any time he fails to comply with these stipulations with regard to wages, the authority may then pay the employees the difference and recover this from the contractor, and the latter is required to keep proper wages books and time sheets, which shall be open to inspection by the officers of the authority.

All this may sound very complicated, and the officers, speaking rapidly at meetings, may make it seem more so, but the duty of the individual member is to see that the matter is openly and honestly dealt with, and that proper value is obtained for the money to be expended. To do this there should be no hesitation in asking questions, however naïve they may appear. Chairmen sometimes get querulous and testy with apparently simple questions, but they should then be reminded gently and firmly that the member has a duty to perform, which he cannot do if he does not fully understand the position. Similarly, officers should be pursued and pinned down by questions addressed to them through the chairman if there is the slightest doubt in a member's mind. There is sometimes a misplaced loyalty to "our" officers, which restrains awkward questions from being asked. This is quite wrong, and a conscientious officer will be the first to admit that he appreciates cross-examination. A flock of sheep looks very well in a field, but it is out of place in a board-room.

APPENDIX I

SPECIMEN STANDING ORDERS

I. MEETINGS

(a) CLASSIFICATION OF MEETINGS, ETC.

Ordinary Meetings

1. The regular ordinary meetings of the Board shall be held on Wednesdays on dates to be fixed according to a programme drawn up in the month of March in each year.

Extraordinary Meetings

2. (i) The Chairman may call a meeting of the Board at any time.
   (ii) If the Chairman refuses to call a meeting after a requisition for that purpose signed by six members has been presented to him, or if, without so refusing, the Chairman does not call a meeting within seven days after such a requisition has been presented to him, any six members may forthwith call a meeting.

Chairman and Vice-Chairman

3. (i) At any meeting of the Board the Chairman, if present, shall preside.
   (ii) If the Chairman is absent from the meeting, the Vice-Chairman, if present, shall preside.
   (iii) If both the Chairman and Vice-Chairman are absent, such member as the members present shall choose, shall preside.

Notice of Meetings

4. Three clear days at least before a meeting a summons to attend the meeting, specifying the business proposed to be transacted thereat and signed by the Chairman or by the Secretary, shall be left at or sent by post to the usual place of residence of every member.

Provided that want of service of the notice or summons on any member shall not affect the validity of any meeting: provided also that, in the case of a meeting called by members in default of the Chairman, the summons shall be signed by those members and no business shall be transacted at the meeting other than that specified in the summons.

(b) BUSINESS AT MEETINGS—GENERAL

Voting

5. Every question at a meeting shall be determined by a majority of the votes of the members present and voting on the question, and in the case of an equality of votes, the person presiding at the meeting shall have a second or casting vote.

Register

6. The names of the members present at a meeting shall be recorded.

Quorum

7. No business shall be transacted at a meeting unless at least one-fourth of the whole number of members are present.

Minutes

8. The minutes of the proceedings of a meeting shall be drawn up and entered in a book or other permanent record kept for that purpose, and, at the next ensuing meeting, shall be submitted for approval as a correct record, and signed by the person presiding thereat.

(c) MOTIONS AND AMENDMENTS

Notices of Motion

9. Subject to the provisions of S.O. 11, a member of the Board desiring to move a motion shall send a notice thereof at least seven clear days before the meeting to the Secretary, who shall insert in the agenda for the meeting all notices so received subject to the same being in order. This paragraph shall not prevent any motion being moved without notice on any business mentioned on the agenda for the meeting.

Withdrawal of Motions or Amendments

10. A motion or amendment once moved and seconded may be withdrawn by the proposer with the concurrence of the seconder and the consent of the Board.

Motion to Rescind a Resolution

11. Notice of motion to rescind any resolution (or the general substance of any resolution) which has been passed within the preceding six calendar months shall bear the signature of the member who gives it and also the signatures of four other members, and before considering any such motion of which notice shall have been given, the Board may refer the matter to an appropriate Committee for their recommendation. When any such motion has been disposed of by the Board it shall not be competent for any member to propose a motion to the same effect within a further period of six calendar months. This order shall not apply to motions moved in pursuance of the report or recommendations of a Committee.

(d) CONDUCT OF DEBATE

Chairman's Ruling

12. The decision of the Chairman of the meeting on the questions of order, relevancy and regularity, and his interpretation of the Standing Orders shall be final.

Manner of Voting

13. (i) All questions put to the vote shall, at the discretion of the Chairman, be determined by oral expression or by show of hands, provided that, upon any question the Chairman may direct, or it may be proposed, seconded and carried that a vote be taken by paper ballot.

(ii) If at least seven members so request, the voting on any question may be recorded so as to show how each member present and voting gave his vote.

(iii) If a member so requests, his vote shall be recorded by name.

(iv) In no circumstances may an absent member vote by proxy.

Motion to "Proceed to Next Business", etc.

14. Any member may move "that the Board do now proceed to the next business", or that "the Board do now adjourn", or that "the question be now put", or that "the debate be now adjourned", on the seconding of which the Chairman, if he is of the opinion that the question before the Board has been sufficiently discussed, shall put the motion to the vote.

If the motion that "the question be now put" be carried, the Chairman shall call on the proposer of the original motion to reply, and, after such reply the original motion and any amendments thereto shall be put forthwith to the Board.

(*e*) INTEREST OF MEMBERS IN CONTRACTS AND OTHER MATTERS

15. If any member of the Board has any pecuniary interest, direct or indirect, in any contract or proposed contract or other matter and is present at a meeting of the Board at which the contract or other matter is the subject of consideration, he shall at the meeting, as soon as practicable after the commencement thereof, disclose the fact, and shall not take part in the consideration or discussion of, or vote on any question with respect to, the contract or proposed contract or other matter and shall retire from such meeting unless the Board invite him to remain.

If any question should arise as to what in any circumstances amounts to a direct or indirect pecuniary interest, the Chairman shall adjudicate on the issue and his decision shall be final.

II. CUSTODY OF COMMON SEAL AND SEALINGS OF DOCUMENTS

(*a*) CUSTODY OF SEAL

16. The common seal of the Board shall be kept in the custody of the Secretary.

(*b*) SEALING OF DOCUMENTS

17. No document shall be sealed except in pursuance of a resolution of the Board or of a Committee to which the Board have by resolution referred and delegated their powers in that behalf.

(*c*) ATTESTATION OF SEALINGS

18. The seal shall be affixed in the presence of two members of the Board and of the Secretary to the Board or his deputy, or some other person approved by resolution of the Board and shall be attested by them.

(*d*) REGISTER OF SEALINGS

19. The Secretary to the Board shall keep a register in which he or his deputy or some other person approved by resolution of the Board shall enter a record of the sealing of every document and every such entry shall be signed by the members of the Board present when the document is sealed. The entries in the register shall be consecutively numbered.

III. COMMITTEES/SUB-COMMITTEES

(*a*) APPOINTMENT OF COMMITTEES/SUB-COMMITTEES

20. The Board shall appoint a Finance Committee and may appoint such other Committees as they consider necessary to carry out the work of the Board and may at any time dissolve or alter the membership of Committees.

(*b*) COMPOSITION OF COMMITTEES

21. The Chairman and Vice-Chairman of the Board shall be *ex officio* a member of every Committee appointed by the Board.

(*c*) PROCEEDINGS IN COMMITTEE TO BE CONFIDENTIAL

22. A member of a Committee shall not disclose a matter dealt with by, or brought before, the Committee without its permission until the Committee shall have reported to the Board or shall otherwise have concluded action on that matter.

Provided that a member of the Board or a member of a Committee shall not disclose any matter reported to the Board or otherwise dealt with by the Committee notwithstanding that the matter has been reported or action has been concluded, if the Board or Committee shall resolve that it is confidential.

(d) Election of Chairman of Committee

23. Every Committee shall, unless its terms of reference provide otherwise, at its first meeting, before proceeding to any other business, elect a Chairman, and, if it so desires, a Vice-Chairman for the year.

(e) SPECIAL MEETINGS OF COMMITTEE

24. The Secretary shall summon any Committee on the request of its Chairman, or on the requisition in writing of one-fourth of the members of the Committee.

(f) SUB-COMMITTEES

25. Every Committee may appoint Sub-Committees for the discussion of any part of the business of the Committee as they may think fit.

(g) QUORUM

26. Except where approved by the Board business shall not be transacted at any meeting of any Committee or Sub-Committee of the Board unless at least one-fourth of the whole number of the Committee or Sub-Committee is present. Provided that in no case shall the quorum of the Committee or Sub-Committee be less than two members.

(h) STANDING ORDERS TO APPLY TO COMMITTEES

27. The Standing Orders of the Board so far as they are applicable shall, *mutatis mutandis*, apply to Committee meetings.

IV. APPOINTMENTS OF OFFICERS, ETC.

(a) CANVASSING OF, AND RECOMMENDATIONS BY, MEMBERS

28. (i) Canvassing of members of the Board or any Committee of the Board for any appointment under the Board shall disqualify the candidate for such appointment.

   (ii) A member of the Board shall not solicit for any person any appointment under the Board or recommend any person for such appointment; but this paragraph of this Standing Order shall not preclude a member from giving a written testimonial of a candidate's ability, experience, or character for submission to the Board.

(b) RELATIVES OF MEMBERS OR OFFICERS

29. Candidates for any appointment under the Board shall, when making application, disclose in writing to the Board whether to their knowledge they are related to any member or the holder of any senior office under the Board. A candidate who purposely and deliberately conceals such information shall be disqualified for such appointment and, if appointed, shall be liable to dismissal without notice. Every member and senior officer of the Board shall disclose to the Board any relationship known to him to exist between himself and a candidate for an appointment of which he is aware. It shall be the duty of the Secretary to the Board to report to the Board any such disclosure made.

   Where the relationship to a member of the Board is disclosed the Standing Order headed "Interest of Members in Contracts and Other Matters" (S.O. 15) shall apply.

   Two persons shall be deemed to be related if they are husband and wife or if either of the two or the spouse of either of them is the son or daughter or grandson or grand-daughter or brother or sister or nephew or niece of the other, or of the spouse of the other.

(c) Interest of Officers in Contracts

30.   If it comes to the knowledge of an officer of the Board that a contract in which he has any pecuniary interest, whether direct or indirect, not being a contract to which he is himself a party, has been, or is proposed to be, entered into by the Board he shall, as soon as practicable, give notice in writing to the Board of the fact that he is interested therein.

In the case of married persons living together, the interest of one spouse shall, if known to the other, be deemed to be also the interest of that spouse.

V. CONTRACTS

Duty to Comply with Standing Orders

31.   (a) Every contract, whether made by the Board or by a Committee of the Board to which the power of making contracts shall have been delegated, shall comply with these Standing Orders, and no exception from any of the following provisions of these Standing Orders shall be made otherwise than by direction of the Board or in an emergency by such a Committee as aforesaid.

(b) Every exception made by a Committee to which the power of making contracts has been delegated shall be reported to the Board and the report shall specify the emergency justifying the exception.

(c) Any exception from any of the provisions of these Standing Orders shall be noted and the reasons for such exception shall be recorded in the minutes of the Board.

Estimates

32.   Before inviting tenders for the execution of any work the Board shall obtain an estimate in writing of the probable expense of executing such work from the appropriate officers and of the subsequent running costs.

Tenders to be Invited

33.   Except as otherwise provided under the Standing Orders tenders shall be obtained and contracts shall be entered into for the following : —

(i) construction, repair, or maintenance of buildings;

(ii) engineering works whether civil, mechanical, or electrical [not included in item (i)];

(iii) supply of goods, materials, or manufactured articles;

(iv) rendering of services involving employment of manual labour.

Obtaining of Tenders

34.   (a) An approved list of contractors for building and engineering works shall be maintained and shall include all firms who have applied for permission to tender and as to whose capacity, conditions of labour, etc., the Board are satisfied and who have for at least three months immediately preceding the application complied with the Fair Wages Resolution passed by the House of Commons on the 14th October, 1946. The approved list shall be reviewed by the Board in alternate years after notice has been given by advertisement in the public press, provided that casual applications for inclusion in the list received during a year shall be considered by the Board at the end of each year.

(b) (i) An opportunity shall be given to all contractors on the approved list to state whether they wish to tender for building and engineering works which are estimated to cost more than £20,000, and which are within the contractors' declared capacity and limits of operation.

(ii) Invitations to tender shall be issued to a limited number of firms from those asking to be considered in accordance with the following scale : —

Contract Sum	Limitation to
Up to £1,000	One or more firms (provided that competitive quotations are obtained wherever possible).
Above £1,000 and up to £5,000	3 firms
Above £5,000 and up to £1 million	6 firms
Above £1 million ...	3 firms

(The number of firms may be varied at the Board's discretion to take account of special circumstances.)

(iii) For works estimated to cost up to £20,000 tenderers shall be selected after reference to the approved list but in accordance with the scale set out in (ii) above.

(iv) The selection of firms to tender for works estimated to cost more than £40,000 shall be made by an *ad hoc* Committee to be appointed by the Board.

(v) The power to make selection of tenderers for works estimated to cost more than £1,000 and up to £40,000 shall be delegated to the Chairman or in his absence the Vice-Chairman of the Board or (in the case of delegated works) to Committees.

(vi) The Officers shall be required in making recommendations for the selection of tenderers to ensure that work is as evenly distributed as possible between all firms on the list which are qualified in accordance with (i) above.

(c) For the supply of goods and services competitive quotations shall, wherever possible, be obtained, provided that direct orders may be placed where the estimated cost does not exceed £20.

(d) Notwithstanding the provisions of the above sub-clauses the Board, instead of inviting tenders from contractors on the approved list for any work, may invite tenders after advertisement in the local, national, or trade Press as thought fit.

Disposals (other than Land and Buildings)

35. Unless tenders are invited, quotations shall be obtained for the disposal of articles by the Board.

The Board or Committee to which has been delegated powers for disposal may in any particular case order that quotations shall be invited by public advertisement.

This Standing Order shall not apply to the disposal of:—

(i) Fixtures and fittings, machinery and old materials in respect of any of which a fair price can be obtained only by negotiation or sale by auction; or

(ii) obsolete or condemned articles and stores under conditions prescribed by the Board.

Submission of Tenders

36. No tender shall be received except in a plain sealed envelope which shall bear the word "Tender" followed by the subject to which it relates, and if desired, the latest date and time for receipt of such tender, but shall not bear any name or mark indicating the sender.

Such envelopes shall be addressed to the Secretary to the Board and shall remain in the custody of the Secretary until the time appointed for their opening.

Provided that the Board may authorise a Committee to receive tenders on their behalf in accordance with the procedure laid down by the Standing Orders of such Committee.

Opening of Tenders

37.   At some convenient time after the latest time for the receipt of tenders, they shall be opened in the presence of the Secretary or his deputy (or other person authorised on their behalf by the Board) in the presence of the Treasurer or Deputy Treasurer.

Every tender and every price alteration appearing on a tender shall be initialled by the officers present at the opening and particulars of the tenders opened, including the sum mentioned therein, shall be entered on a schedule which shall similarly be initialled.

Provided that the Board may authorise a Committee to open tenders on their behalf in accordance with the procedure laid down by the Standing Orders of such Committee.

Acceptance of Tenders

38.   A tender other than the lowest tender, if payment is to be made by the Board, or other than the highest, if payment is to be received by the Board, shall not be accepted unless for good and sufficient reason the Board decide otherwise and record that decision in their minutes.

Form of Contract

39.   (*a*) Every contract (i) for the supply of goods or services which is likely to exceed £500 (ii) for the execution of works which is likely to exceed £1,500 in value or amount shall be embodied in a formal document which shall conform to these Standing Orders (hereinafter referred to in the Standing Orders as a "formal contract"), and which shall be signed on behalf of the Board by the Secretary or his Deputy.

   (*b*) Every contract shall specify: —

      (i) the work, materials, matters, or things to be furnished or done;

      (ii) the price to be paid, with a statement of discount or other deductions if any: and where practicable;

      (iii) the time or times within which the contract is to be performed.

   (*c*) Contracts for the execution of works may provide for liquidated and ascertained damages to be paid by the contractor in the event of the terms of the contract not being duly performed, and the Board may at their discretion require and take sufficient security for the due performance of every such contract. Where provision for such damages or security is required, the form of tender should contain a specific undertaking to provide the same if the tender is accepted.

   (*d*) Contracts may provide that the contractor or sub-contractor shall not assign or underlet the contract or sub-contract or any part of it without the written consent of the Board or their authorised officers.

British Standards

40. All formal contracts, where a standard issued by the British Standards Institution is current at the date of the tender and is appropriate, shall require that goods and materials used in their execution shall be in accordance with that standard.

Inducements

41. In every formal contract a clause shall be inserted to secure that the Board shall be entitled to cancel the contract and to recover from the contractor the amount of any loss resulting from such cancellation, if the contractor shall have offered or given or agreed to give to any person any gift or consideration of any kind as an inducement or reward for doing or forbearing to do or having done or forborne to do any action in relation to the obtaining or execution of the contract or any other contract with the Board or if the like acts shall have been done by any person employed by him or acting on his behalf (whether with or without the knowledge of the contractor), or if in relation to any contract with the Board the contractor or any person employed by him or acting on his behalf shall have committed an offence under the Prevention of Corruption Acts, 1889 to 1916.

Default by Contractor

42. In every formal contract for the supply of goods or materials a clause shall be inserted to secure that, should the contractor fail to deliver the goods or materials or any portion thereof within the time or times specified in the contract, the Board, without prejudice to any other remedy for breach of contract, shall be at liberty to determine the contract either wholly or to the extent of such default and to purchase other goods of the same or similar description to make good (*a*) such default or (*b*) in the event of the contract being wholly determined the balance of the goods remaining to be delivered. The clause should further secure that any excess of the purchase price over the contract price appropriate to such default or balance shall be recoverable from the contractor.

Fair Wages Resolution

43. In every formal contract for the execution of work or the supply of goods or materials a clause shall be inserted to secure that the contractor shall in respect of all persons employed by him (whether in execution of this contract or otherwise) in every factory, workshop, or place occupied or used by him for the execution of the contract comply with the following conditions of the Fair Wages Resolution passed by the House of Commons on the 14th October, 1946, namely: —

1. (*a*) The contractor shall pay rates of wages and observe hours and conditions of labour not less favourable than those established for the trade or industry in the district where the work is carried out by machinery of negotiation or arbitration to which the parties are organisations of employers' and trade unions' representatives respectively of substantial proportions of the employers and workers engaged in the trade or industry in the district;

   (*b*) In the absence of any rates of wages, hours, or conditions of labour so established the contractor shall pay rates of wages and observe hours and conditions of labour which are not less favourable than the general level of wages, hours, and conditions observed by other employers whose general circumstances in the trade or industry in which the contractor is engaged are similar.

2. The contractor shall recognise the freedom of his workpeople to be members of trade unions.

3. The contractor shall at all times during the continuance of the contract display, for the information of his workpeople in every factory,

workshop, or place occupied or used by him for the execution of the contract, a copy of the Fair Wages Resolution.

4. The contractor shall be responsible for the observance of this clause by sub-contractors employed in the execution of the contract, and shall if required notify the Board of the names and addresses of all such sub-contractors.

5. In the event of any question arising as to whether the foregoing conditions of the Fair Wages Resolution are being observed, the question shall, if not otherwise disposed of, be referred by the Ministry of Labour and National Service to an independent tribunal for decision.

Contractor's Compliance with Fair Wages Resolution

44. Before entering into a formal contract for the execution of work or the supply of goods or materials, the Board shall obtain from the contractor an assurance that to the best of his knowledge and belief he has complied with the general conditions of the Fair Wages Resolution passed by the House of Commons on the 14th October, 1946, for at least three months immediately preceding the date of the tender.

Failure to Comply with Fair Wages Resolution

45. In every formal contract for the execution of work or the supply of goods or materials clauses to the following effect shall be inserted:—

(a) If the contractor at any time or times or from time to time during the continuance of the contract fails to pay to any person or persons employed by him in or about the execution of the contract, wages in conformity with the conditions of the Fair Wages Resolution passed by the House of Commons on the 14th October, 1946, the Board may, without in any way prejudicing or affecting any of their rights, powers, and remedies under the contract in respect of any breach of contract involved, pay to the employee or employees concerned the amount of the difference between the sum or sums (if any) which such employee or employees may have received from the contractor as wages, and the sum or sums which the employee or employees should have received had the contractor performed and observed the said conditions and the Board may recover from the contractor as a debt due to the Board the amount so paid by the Board as aforesaid.

(b) The contractor shall keep proper wages books and time sheets showing the wages paid to and the time worked (distinguishing between normal time and overtime) by each person employed in and about the execution of the contract, and such wages books and time sheets shall be produced whenever required for the inspection of any officer authorised by the Board.

VI.   MISCELLANEOUS

(a) Variation or Suspension of Standing Orders

46. (i) Any motion to vary or revoke any one or more of these Standing Orders shall, when proposed and seconded, stand adjourned without discussion to the next meeting of the Board.

(ii) Any one or more of the Standing Orders may, either after motion on notice, or, in any case of urgency, on motion without notice, be suspended at any meeting so far as regards any business at such meeting, provided that there are seven members present, and that not less than two-thirds of the members present vote for such suspension.

(*b*) STANDING ORDERS TO BE GIVEN TO MEMBERS

47. A copy of these Standing Orders shall be given to each member of the Board by the Secretary.

(*c*) SIGNING OF DOCUMENTS

48. Where any documents will be a necessary step in legal proceedings on behalf of the Board, it shall, unless any enactment otherwise requires or authorises, or the Board shall have given the necessary authority to some other person for the purpose of such proceedings, be signed by the Secretary to the Board.

VII. INTERPRETATION

Interpretation of Standing Orders
49. The Chairman of the Board shall be the final authority in the interpretation of Standing Orders on which he shall be advised by the Secretary.

APPENDIX II

It will be appreciated that the agenda for a meeting of any important body may comprise 35-40 items, many of which are of considerable magnitude. The following fictitious agenda and minutes merely illustrate how the business of a meeting should be set down.

SPECIMEN AGENDA

THE A——— REGIONAL HOSPITAL BOARD

Meeting to be held at Fincham Hospital, Littletown, on Monday, 29th August, 1960, at 10.30 a.m.

Agenda:

1. Apologies for absence.
2. Minutes of the meeting of the Board held on 28th July, 1960.
3. Matters arising from the minutes.
4. Appointment of Assistant Secretary to the Board. Report of Selection Committee.
5. Estimates for new boiler house at Allerham Hospital.
6. Grants for study leave.
7. Appointments systems for out-patient departments. Senior Administrative Medical Officer to report.
8. Any other business.

APPENDIX III

SPECIMEN MINUTES

Minutes of Meeting
of the
A———— Regional Hospital Board
held at Fincham Hospital, Littletown,
on Monday, 29th August, 1960.

Present

    Chairman: Mr. A————.
    Members: Mr. B————.
            Dr. C   .
            Mr. D————.
            Mr. E————.
            Mr. F————.
            Mr. G————.
            Dr. H————.
            Mrs. I————.
            Mr. J————.
            Col. K————.
            Mr. L————,
            Mr. M————.
            Dr. N————.
            Mr. O————.
            Professor P————.
    Officers: Dr. R————. Senior Administrative Medical Officer.
            Mr. S————. Secretary to the Board.
            Mr. T————. Treasurer.
            Mr. U————. Architect.

Apologies for absence were received from General V————, Professor W————, Dr. X————, Mr. Y————, Mrs. Z————.

1. *Minutes of previous meeting.*

The minutes of the meeting held on 28th July, 1960, having been circulated, were taken as read and signed by the Chairman.

2. *Matters arising from the minutes.*

It was reported that the land adjoining the ———— Hospital is no longer available for acquisition.

3. *Appointment of Assistant Secretary to the Board.*

The Chairman of the Selection Committee reported that, after having interviewed four candidates from a short list, the Committee recommends the appointment of Mr. Robert A————, at present Secretary to the B———— Hospital Management Committee, as Assistant Secretary to the Board.

    Resolved that

         Mr. Robert A———— be appointed Assistant Secretary to the Board.

4. *Estimates for new boiler house at Allerham Hospital.*
Three tenders were received for this work.
Resolved that
    the tender of Messrs. B——— and C——— in the sum of £13,210 9s.
be accepted, and that a formal document under seal be prepared for the
carrying out of the work.

5. *Grants for study leave.*
After a lengthy discussion on this subject, in which Professor P———
emphasised the particular importance of post-graduate study,
Resolved that
    the Secretary to the Board ask the appropriate officers of the Ministry
of Health for further clarification on the subject of financial assistance
for study leave.

6. *Appointments systems for out-patient departments.*
The Senior Administrative Medical Officer reported that, having taken
into consideration the numbers of patients to be seen in the various out-
patient departments, the distances patients travelled to hospitals, and the
general transport services available, and having discussed the subject with
the consultants concerned, he was of the opinion that satisfactory appointments systems could be introduced.
Resolved that
    the Hospital Management Committees be asked to introduce appoint-
ments systems in agreement with the consultant medical staffs and that
these be put into operation for a trial period of twelve months, and that
at the end of this time the matter be again brought forward for the
consideration of the Board.

7. *Any other business.*
The question of entertainment for patients at Christmas was raised.
Resolved that
    this matter be placed on the agenda for the next meeting.

There being no other business the meeting closed at 12.45 p.m.

Date of Next Meeting: 27th September, 1960.

BIBLIOGRAPHY

Anderson, Sir John (Lord Waverley), *Administrative Technique in the Public Services* (Birkbeck College, University of London, 1949).

Brech, E. F. L., *Organisation: the Framework of Management* (Longmans, Green & Co., 1965).

Principles and Practice of Management (Pitman, 1963).

Bridges, Lord, *The Treasury* (George Allen & Unwin, 1966).

Bridges, Sir E., *Portrait of a Profession* (C.U.P., 1950).

Collison, Robert L., *Modern Business Filing and Archives* (Benn & de Graff, 1963).

Craig, Sir John, *History of Red Tape* (Macdonald & Evans, 1955).

Ennis, R. W., *Introduction to Accountability* (Lyon Grant & Green, 1967).

Franks, Baron, *Experience of a University Teacher in the Civil Service* (O.U.P., 1947).

Gladden, E. N., *Introduction to Public Administration* (Staples, 1966).

Hankey, M. P. A. (Lord Hankey), *Science and Art of Government* (O.U.P., 1951).

Helmore, L. M., *The District Auditor* (Macdonald & Evans, 1961).

H.M.S.O., *Britain, an Official Handbook*.

Hooper, Sir F. C., *Management Survey in the Public Services* (Pitman, 1961).

Jackson, R. M., *Machinery of Local Government* (Macmillan, 1965).

Jennings, Sir Ivor, *Cabinet Government* (C.U.P., 1961).

Johnston, Sir Alexander, *The Inland Revenue* (George Allen & Unwin, 1965).

Lewis, E. M. R., and Maude, A. E., *Professional People* (Phoenix House, 1952).

Mackenzie, W. J. M., and Grove, J. W., *Central Administration in Britain* (Longmans, 1957).

Milward, G. E., *Organisation and Methods* (Macmillan & Co., 1967).

Mountford, Sir J., "Universities of the United Kingdom", *Commonwealth Universities Year Book, 1963.*

British Universities (Oxford Paperbacks, Univ. Ser. 14), 1966.

National Council of Social Service, *CANS (Citizens Advice Notes).*

Royal Institute of Public Administration, *Making of an Administrator* (Editor, A. Dunsire) (Manchester U.P., 1956).

Shaw, S., and Smith, E. D., *Law of Meetings* (Macdonald & Evans, 1956).

Sisson, C. H., *Spirit of British Administration* (Faber, 1966).

Urwick, L., *Pattern of Management* (Pitman, 1956).

Elements of Administration (Pitman, 1955).

Wade, E. C. S., and Phillips, G. G., *Constitutional Law* (Longmans, 1965).

Wade, H. W. R., *Administrative Law* (Clarendon Press, 1967).

Warren, J. H., *English Local Government System* (Allen & Unwin, 1965).

Wheare, Sir Kenneth Clinton, *Government by Committee* (O.U.P, 1955).

Machinery of Government (Clarendon Press, 1945).

INDEX

INDEX

PRINTED IN GREAT BRITAIN BY UNIVERSITY TUTORIAL PRESS LTD, FOXTON

NEAR CAMBRIDGE